THE CATHOLIC UNIVERSITY OF AMERICA
CANON LAW STUDIES
No. 159

The Desecration and Violation of Churches

AN HISTORICAL SYNOPSIS AND COMMENTARY

BY

JOHN THEOPHILUS GULCZYNSKI, J.C.L.
Priest of the Diocese of Dallas

A DISSERTATION

Submitted to the Faculty of Canon Law of the Catholic University of America in Partial Fulfillment of the Requirements for the Degree of

DOCTOR OF CANON LAW

THE CATHOLIC UNIVERSITY OF AMERICA
WASHINGTON, D. C.
1942

NIHIL OBSTAT:
CLEMENS V. BASTNAGEL, J.U.D., S.T.L.,
Censor Deputatus
Washingtonii, die 13ª iunii, 1942

IMPRIMATUR:
✠ JOSEPHUS PATRITIUS LYNCH, D.D.,
Episcopus Dallasensis
Dallasii, die 16ª augusti, 1942

PRINTED IN THE UNITED STATES OF AMERICA
BY THE WATKINS PRINTING CO., BALTIMORE

TABLE OF CONTENTS

PART II — COMMENTARY

FOREWORD

Churches are endowed with a sacred character that is given to them when they are dedicated to the worship of God by the liturgical rite of consecration or blessing. The celebration of divine services is permitted in a church as long as that sacred character has not been lost by desecration or defiled by violation. It is the purpose of this work to offer a study of the canonical legislation concerning the desecration and violation of churches.

The work is divided into two parts, one a historical synopsis and the other a canonical commentary. In the first part an attempt is made to trace the origin of the laws regarding the desecration and violation of churches, and to point out the various changes effected in the enactment of these laws along with the various interpretations that were given to them in the course of their successive development. The second part of the dissertation is a commentary of the law as it is found at the present time in the Code of Canon Law. An explanation is given of the legal factors and the conditions under which the desecration and violation of churches is brought about.

The writer takes this opportunity to express his gratitude to the Most Reverend Joseph P. Lynch, D.D., LL.D., Bishop of Dallas, for the opportunity offered for advanced study, to the members of the Faculty of the School of Canon Law for their assistance and direction in the preparation of this work and to all others, especially the Reverend Walter J. Canavan, M.A., Litt.D., J.C.D., who have in any way helped to make this work possible.

INTRODUCTION

It is necessary at the very outset to clarify the meaning of the terms that are to be used in this work, in order to avoid the confusion which would inevitably arise from an improper understanding of the terms. The term "*desecration*" will be used throughout the work for the lack of a more suitable English equivalent of the Latin expression "*exsecratio.*" For the purpose of uniformity the term "*violation*" will be used to convey the idea of the Latin expressions "*pollutio*" and "*violatio.*" Other expressions that do not readily lend themselves to a literal translation into English will be used in the original Latin terminology.

Some modern authors [1] use the terms desecration and violation as having identical meanings. It is the firm conviction of the present writer that the two terms cannot and should not be used synonymously. The term desecration is derived from *de* and *sacrare* [2] and means the removal of the sacred character from a person or a thing. Violation, on the other hand, is a temporary suspension of the effects of the consecration or blessing of a church, which suspension is caused by certain acts, specified in law, which have been committed in the church, but this suspension of effects does not cause the church to lose its consecration or blessing.[3] The terms present two distinct concepts and, therefore, should not be used interchangeably.

The desecration of a church may be defined as the removal of the sacred character which was given to the church through its consecration or blessing.[4] In other words, the desecration of a church is the loss of its consecration or blessing.[5] The present Code

[1] Augustine, *A Commentary on the New Code of Canon Law* (8 vols., St. Louis: Herder, Vol. VI, 3. ed., *Administrative Law,* 1931), VI, 35; Ayrinhac, *Administrative Legislation in the New Code of Canon Law* (New York: Longmans, Green & Co., 1930), p. 21; Beste, *Introductio in Codicem* (Collegeville, Minn.: St. John's Abbey Press, 1938), p. 564.

[2] *Thesaurus Linguae Latinae* (Lipsiae, 1900-), v. "desecratio."

[3] Coronata, *De Locis et Temporibus Sacris* (Taurini: Marietti, 1922), n. 27.

[4] Wernz-Vidal, *Ius Canonicum* (7 vols. in 8, Romae: apud Aedes Universitatis Gregorianae, 1923-1938), IV, pars I *(De Rebus),* n. 365.

[5] Ojetti, *Synopsis Rerum Moralium et Iuris Pontificii* (Romae: 1899), v. "exsecratio"; Many, *Praelectiones de Locis Sacris* (Parisiis: 1904), n. 25.

of Canon Law mentions three ways by which a church may lose its consecration or blessing, namely: a) by the total destruction of the church; b) by the collapse of the major part of the walls; c) by the conversion of the church to secular purposes through the local ordinary in accordance with the rules given in canon 1187.[6]

The desecration of a church does not cause the desecration of the immovable or fixed altars in the church; nor does the desecration of an altar desecrate the church in which it is erected.[7] The reason for this is that the consecration of a church and the consecration of an altar are two distinct consecrations and therefore exist independently of each other.[8] An altar, however, would become desecrated along with the desecration of a church if some part of the walls of the church, or some other object, should fall on the altar in such a manner as to cause the table of the altar to be moved from its support, or if the table itself were considerably broken.[9]

It is forbidden to hold religious services in a new church before it has been solemnly consecrated or at least dedicated to divine worship by a blessing.[10] It is likewise forbidden to hold religious services in a church which has lost its consecration or blessing, unless the church has been repaired and consecrated or blessed again in the same manner as should be done in the case of a newly built church.[11]

6 Canon 1170.

7 Canon 1200, § 4.

8 Coronata, *De Locis et Temporibus Sacris,* n. 117; Many, *De Locis Sacris,* n. 123; Barbosa, *Iuris Ecclesiastici Universi Libri Tres* (Lugduni: 1660), lib. II, cap. VII, n. 23 (henceforth this work will be referred to as *Ius Ecclesiasticum Universum);* Bliley, *Altars According to the New Code of Canon Law,* Catholic University of America Canon Law Studies, n. 38 (Washington: The Catholic University of America, 1927), p. 96; cf. also *Pontificale Romanum Summorum Pontificum iussu editum a Benedicto XIV et Leone XIII Pont. Max. recognitum et castigatum* (Ratisbonae, Neo Eboraci et Cincinnati: 1891), tit. *De Altaris Consecratione, quae fit sine Ecclesiae dedicatione.*

9 Canon 1200, § 1, 2°.

10 Canon 1165, § 1.

11 Wernz, *Ius Decretalium* (6 vols. in 10, Romae et Prati: 1905-1914), III (Romae: 1908), n. 441; Coronata, *De Locis et Temporibus Sacris,* n. 26, 4°; De Angelis, *Praelectiones Iuris Canonici ad methodum Decretalium Gregorii IX exactae* (4 vols. in 6, Romae: 1877-1887), lib. III, tit. 40, n. 4.

The violation of a church is defined as an injury inflicted by certain acts specified in law which blemish the sacred character of a church and render it unfit for divine services until the blemish is removed by the sacred rite of reconciliation.[12] The violation of a church does not cause it to lose its consecration or blessing, but all sacred functions are forbidden to be celebrated in the church until the rite of reconciliation is performed.[13]

The acts that bring about the violation of a church are enumerated in canon 1172. They are four in number: a) the crime of homicide; b) the injurious and grave shedding of blood; c) the impious and sordid uses to which a church has been converted; d) the burial of an infidel or of a person whose excommunication is attended with a declaratory or condemnatory sentence. Furthermore, before a church can become violated the same canon presupposes that the violative acts were certain, notorious and committed in the church proper.

Strictly taken there is no special violation of an altar distinct from the violation of a church. This is apparent from the *Roman Pontifical* and the *Roman Ritual*, neither of which gives a special rite for the reconciliation of a violated altar. The altar, however, is affected indirectly, for it is forbidden to celebrate Mass upon the altar of a violated church until the rite of reconciliation of the church has been performed.[14]

[12] De Angelis, *loc. cit.*

[13] Wernz, *Ius Decretalium*, III, n. 442; Gasparri, *Tractatus Canonicus de Sanctissima Eucharistia* (2 vols., Parisiis et Lugduni: 1897), I, n. 243; Schmalzgrueber, *Ius Ecclesiasticum Universum* (5 vols. in 12, Romae: 1843-1845), lib. III, tit. 40, n. 63.

[14] Cf. Many, *De Locis Sacris*, n. 125; Coronata, *De Locis et Temporibus Sacris*, n. 117; Bliley, *Altars*, p. 96.

PART I
HISTORY

Chapter I
CHURCHES

Article I. Origin

The word *church* as used in this work does not mean the society of the faithful which constitutes the mystical body of Christ, but rather "a sacred building dedicated to divine worship, principally for the purpose that it may be used by all the faithful for the public exercise of divine worship." [1]

The first Christians did not have churches in the sense in which they are understood today; nevertheless there were certain places set apart in which the Christians assembled for divine worship. These primitive churches were ordinary private houses, such as the one having the upper room, so often mentioned in Holy Scripture, where Matthias was chosen to replace Judas,[2] and where the Apostles were assembled in prayer when the Holy Ghost descended upon them.[3] Possibly this room was used when the Apostles elected and ordained the seven deacons,[4] and it is probable that this was the place where the I Council of Jerusalem was held.[5]

St. Paul in many of his letters[6] saluted the congregations of the faithful that met in the houses of pious Christians who had permitted some part of their dwelling to be used as a place of worship. Such places were considered sacred, and it was demanded that due respect and reverence be given them. St. Paul distinguished between ordinary dwellings and homes which had been converted to

[1] Canon 1161.
[2] Acts, I: 13-26.
[3] Acts, II: 1-4.
[4] Acts, VI: 2-6.
[5] Acts, XV: 6-29.
[6] Rom., XVI: 5; I Cor., XVI: 19; Phil., I: 2.

houses of worship and he rebuked those who showed a lack of proper respect for the latter.[7]

With the spread of Christianity and the consequent increase in the number of the faithful, private homes were given over in their entirety to be used for religious purposes. These buildings not only provided accommodations for the faithful, the catechumens, and the penitents who attended religious services, but also served as a dwelling-place for the bishop and the clergy. Parts of the buildings were used as a refectory, as a dispensary, and particularly as an alms-house for the poor. The part set aside for worship took on a special importance of its own and became separated from the other parts of the building. It came to be known as the house of God (*domus Dei*). It was used exclusively for acts of devotion and religion, and did not allow of anything to be done there that did not reflect some indication of religious piety or have some immediate relation to it. Such a part of the house could be used for religious assemblies, for the election of bishops and of the clergy, for conferences about theological topics, but it could not be utilized as the remaining parts of the house, that is, for eating, drinking, lodging, etc.[8]

It is to be remembered that the Christian religion was proscribed by law from the very beginning until the time of the famous Edict of Toleration given at Milan in the year 313. Hence during the time of the persecutions the Church was not recognized as a legal organization, and thus could not hold any property in its own name. However, Roman law granted legal personality to charitable organizations (*collegia tenuiorum*) and burial associations (*collegia funeraticia*). Therefore, since the Church performed acts of mercy of this kind, land and buildings could become the property of Christian charitable organizations. Legal protection, then, was granted to the property, not because it belonged to the Church, but because it

[7] "Have you not houses for your eating and drinking? Or do you despise the church of God and put to shame the needy? What am I to say to you? Am I to commend you? In this I do not commend you."—I Cor., XI: 22.

[8] Duchesne, *Christian Worship, Its Origin and Evolution* (5. ed., London: MacMillan Co., 1931), 399-400; Bingham, *The Antiquities of the Christian Church* (2 vols., London: 1856), Book VIII, chap. I, sect. 13.

belonged to a legally recognized organization.[9] Such property, however, was subject to confiscation if it was discovered that the membership of the organizations was composed of adherents of the forbidden religion.

The Church, using to its advantage the protection given by law, made use of public churches in addition to private houses for religious purposes. It is recorded by Eusebius [10] that in the time of Pope Cornelius (251-253) there were 44 priests, 7 deacons, 7 subdeacons, 42 acolytes, 52 exorcists, lectors and porters, and 1500 virgins, infirm persons and poor attached to the church at Rome alone. It may be inferred from the aforesaid that it was necessary to have a building of huge proportions to accommodate such a large number at religious functions. With a temporary grant of peace Emperor Gallienus, in the year 260, revoked a prior edict of his predecessor, Valerian, and ordered that all places dedicated to divine worship be returned to the Christians.[11]

One of the more celebrated cases is that of Paul of Samosata (circa 272), who was declared a heretic by the ecclesiastical authorities and consequently deposed from his office. He was ordered to give up the church which he governed in Antioch. Upon his refusal to comply with the order, recourse was made to the emperor, Aurelian, who declared that the church should be returned to the Christian community which was in communion with the bishop of Rome.[12]

Finally, the edict of Milan, issued jointly by Constantine and Licinius, granted absolute freedom of worship to the Christians and declared that the churches and all the property belonging to them, which had been confiscated during the persecutions, should be restored to the Church without hesitation or controversy.[13]

[9] De Rossi, *La Roma Sotteranea Cristiana* (3 vols., Roma: 1864-1877), I, 101-103.

[10] *Historia Ecclesiastica*, VI, 43—Migne, *Patrologiae Cursus Completus, Series Graeca* (161 vols., Parisiis: 1856-1866), XX, 622 (hereafter this work will be referred to as *MPG)*.

[11] Eusebius, *Hist. Eccles.*, VII, 13—MPG, XX, 674.

[12] Eusebius, *Hist. Eccles.*, VII, 30—MPG, XX, 719.

[13] The text of this decree is quoted in full by Lactantius, *De Mortibus*

All of the above mentioned texts give sufficient evidence in testimony of the existence of churches from the very beginning of Christianity and throughout the persecutions. From the time of Constantine onward, with some local exceptions, it is an undeniable historical fact that churches existed unmolested by the secular power.

Article II. Early Appellations

The churches of the early Christians were referred to by various names, the most common of which was *ecclesia* as opposed to the synagogue of the Jews and the temples of the pagans. St. Paul was the first to make use of this expression.[14] Tertullian (c. 160-222/3) made frequent use of it in his many writings,[15] as well as Eusebius when he related the great change brought about in the Roman Empire with the conversion of Constantine to the Catholic faith.[16]

Another very common name was *Dominicum.*[17] St. Cyprian (190-258), Archbishop of Carthage (249-258), applied it not oniy to the church but also to the Lord's Supper.[18] The same name occurred in other Latin writers, as in Rufinus of Aquileia (345-410), who in a historical narrative introduces to his readers the bishop who converted

Persecutorum, c. 48—Migne, *Patrologiae Cursus Completus, Series Latina* (221 vols., Parisiis: 1844-1864), VII, 267-270 (hereafter this work will be referred to as *MPL*).

[14] "Numquid domos non habetis ad manducandum et bibendum? aut *ecclesiam Dei contemnitis?*"—I Cor. XI: 22.

[15] "In ecclesia virginitatem suam abscondant quam extra ecclesiam celant," *De Virginibus Velandis,* cap. 13—*MPL,* II, 907; *De Pudicitia,* cap. 4—*MPL,* II, 987.

[16] "Pulcherrimae et magnificentissimae ecclesiae monumenta exornavit," *De Vita Constantini,* III, 50—*MPG,* XX, 1110.

[17] The Latin *Dominicum* has its origin in the Greek *κυριακόν,* from which is derived the Scotch *kirk,* the German *Kirche,* and the English *church.* Cf. Bingham, *Christian Antiquities,* Book VIII, chap. I, sect. 2; Duchesne, *Christian Worship,* p. 400; Augustine, *A Commentary on the New Code of Canon Law,* VI, 12.

[18] "Locuples et dives es, et Dominicum celebrare te credis, quae corbonam omnino non respicis? quae in Dominicum sine sacrificiis venis; quae partem de sacrificio, quod pauper obtulit, sumis?"—*De opere et eleemosyna,* 15—*MPL,* IV, 613.

a philosopher at the Council of Niceae (325) and addressed himself to the new convert thus: "Arise and follow me to the *Dominicum* and there receive the seal of your faith."[19] St. Jerome (circa 342-420) relates that the famous church of Antioch, which was begun by Constantine and finished and dedicated by Constantius, had the name of *Dominicum aureum* because of its richness and beauty.[20]

Basilica was an expression which was used quite generally after the persecutions to designate a church. Originally among the Romans *basilicae* were the public halls or courts where the magistrates sat to hold trials. Other buildings, such as state houses, went by the same name, but upon the conversion of Constantine many of these were given to the Christians to be used as churches.[21] St. Isidore of Seville (†636)[22] explained that formerly the homes of kings were called *basilicae* because the Greek *βασιλεὺς* meant king, hence the Latin derivation of the word was used to signify a royal home. He related, further, that the term in his time was employed to designate churches because sacrifices were offered in them to God, the King of the universe. St. Ambrose (c. 340-397) in a letter to Emperor Theodosius I (379-395), written in 388, complained of the burning of the *basilicae* by the Jews throughout the Empire during the reign of Emperor Julian (361-363).[23] The term also appears in some of his other works.[24]

Just as the temple of the Jews in Jerusalem was frequently referred to in Sacred Scripture as the house of prayer,[25] so Christian churches, because prayer was one of the principal functions performed

19 Rufinus, *Historia Ecclesiastica*, I, 3—*MPL*, XXI, 470.

20 "In Antiochia Dominicum, quod vocatur Aureum, aedificari coeptum [anno 331]"—*Chronicon*—*MPL*, XXVIII, 677; cf. also the note on this text, as contained in *MPL*, *loc. cit.*

21 De Rossi, *La Roma Sotteranea Cristiana*, III, 460.

22 W. M. Lindsay, *Isidori Hispalensis Episcopi Etymologiarum sive Originum Libri XX* (2 vols. in 1, Oxonii, 1911), lib. XV, cap. 4, n. 11; *MPL*, LXXXII, 545.

23 *Epist. XL*, 15—*MPL*, XVI, 1107.

24 Sermo, *De Basilicis Tradendis, contra Auxentium*—*MPL*, XVI, 1007; *Epist. XX*—*MPL*, XVI, 997.

25 "Domus mea, domus orationis vocabitur"—Matt. XXI, 13.

within them, were termed *oratories* or houses of prayer. Eusebius recorded that Constantine built many oratories throughout the city which bore his name, as well as in the suburbs.[26] Although this term was applied to all churches in the first four centuries, in the following ages it was restricted in its use to private chapels, or to places of worship which were set up for the convenience of private families, and were used only as places of prayer, all religious services being excluded.[27]

It was the common practice in ancient times, as it is today, for people to visit and adorn the graves of their relatives and friends, and thus it was the practice of the Christian communities to honor the martyrs. It became the custom for the entire community to gather annually at or near the grave of a martyr and honor his martyrdom with the celebration of the Eucharistic sacrifice.[28] Later, when the persecutions ceased, many churches were built over the graves of martyrs and were given the distinguishing title of *martyria.* Hence the church built in Rome by Constantine was designated as the *Martyrium Petri et Pauli.*[29] For the same reason, because Jesus Christ was the chief sufferer and great martyr of his own religion, the church built in Jerusalem was called the *Martyrium Salvatoris.*[30] In Constantinople there were erected many oratories and *martyria.* "In this manner [Constantine] honored the memory of the martyrs and simultaneously dedicated to God his city of martyrs." [31]

The name *temple* during the first three centuries was used in connection with the pagan temples, but it was scarcely ever used by Christian writers to designate a Christian church. Whenever the term was used, it was written not in its simple form, but appeared

[26] *De Vita Constantini,* III, 48—MPG, XX, 1107; *Hist. Eccles.,* X, 3—MPG, XX, 846.

[27] "Oratorium orationi tantum est consecratum, in quo nemo aliquid agere debet nisi ad quod factum."—Lindsay, *Isidori Hispalensis Episcopi Etymologiarum sive Originum Libri XX,* lib. XV, cap. 4, n. 4; *MPL,* LXXXII, 544.

[28] Bingham, *Antiquities of the Christian Church,* Book VIII, chap. I, sect. 9; Bliley, *Altars According to the Code of Canon Law,* p. 35.

[29] Socrates, *Historia Ecclesiastica,* IV, 23—MPG, LXVII, 522.

[30] Eusebius, *De Vita Constantini,* IV, 40—MPG, XX, 1188.

[31] Eusebius, *De Vita Constantini,* III, 48—MPG, XX, 1107.

always with some qualification, e. g., *templum Dei.* Lactantius stated that he taught oratory in Bithynia when the temple of God was destroyed, meaning the church of Nicomedia, which was the first that was demolished in the Diocletian persecution.[32] When Christianity became the religion of the State and pagan temples were outlawed, the writers of the following ages did not hesitate to call churches by the name of temples. Eusebius, speaking of the churches that were rebuilt, called them temples.[33] There was no longer any aversion to the word *temple* in the fourth century, for it could no longer be mistaken to mean the temple of the heathen.

ARTICLE III. EARLY CEREMONIES OF DEDICATION

Even though the Christians had churches during the first three centuries, they refrained from performing any acts within them which would attract public attention, for fear of arousing the hostility of the pagans which would have manifested itself in the confiscation of the sacred buildings. Because of this constant fear there is no express testimony to show that any solemn dedication of churches took place during this period. This lack of evidence, however, is no justification for denying that there was a dedication of churches. The mere fact of designating a particular building to be used exclusively for religious purposes was considered its dedication. It is very probable that some appropriate prayers were used to offer thanksgiving to God and to invoke His blessing upon the building and those who were to use it.

The earliest positive evidence of the consecration of churches comes from the fourth century, after peace and freedom of worship were granted to the Christians. Eusebius stated that "it was a desirable sight to behold how the consecration of the newly built churches and the feasts of the dedications were solemnized in every city." [34] To add to the solemnity of the occasion it was not unusual to have a large number of bishops present for the consecration of a church. At the dedication of the church of Antioch, called the

[32] *Divinarum Institutionum Libri VII,* V, cap. 2—*MPL,* VI, 553.
[33] *Hist. Eccles.,* X, 2—MPG, XX, 846.
[34] *Hist. Eccles.,* X, 3—MPG, XX, 847.

Dominicum aureum, 97 bishops were in attendance.[35] The ceremony was of a solemn and public nature, accompanied by panegyrical orations, consisting chiefly of praise and thanksgiving to God for the accomplishment of the holy structure, as is seen from the sermon preached at the consecration of the basilica of Tyre.[36]

Later in the same century the churches which were built over the tombs of the martyrs came to be regarded as endowed with a sanctity peculiar to themselves. Thus the possession of the relics of some saint came to be looked upon as absolutely essential to the sacredness of the building, and the deposition of such relics in or below the altar thenceforth formed an important part of the consecration rite.[37] St. Ambrose seems to be the first to popularize in Italy the custom of placing the relics of martyrs in the churches on the occasion of their consecration. In a letter to his sister, written in 386, he explained that, when he was about to consecrate the basilica at Milan, the people insisted that relics be placed in the church.[38] The relics of SS. Gervase and Protase were not placed in the church during its dedication, because they were not to be had at the time. It was not until later that the relics were discovered and placed beneath the altar of the basilica after great throngs had spent two days venerating the relics and keeping a solemn vigil during the night prior to their deposition.[39] Another example is given in the sermon of St. Ambrose at the consecration of the basilica built by the widow Juliana at Florence in 393. St.

[35] Sozomenus, *Hist. Eccles.*, III, 5—*MPG*, LXVII, 1042.

[36] Eusebius, *Hist. Eccles.*, X, 4—*MPG*, XX, 850.

[37] It is to be noted that the relics which were placed in many of the churches were not necessarily the bodies of the martyrs, but the clothes and other objects which had come in contact with the bodies, and particularly objects which had been soaked in the blood of the martyrs.—Cf. Many, *Praelectiones De Locis Sacris* (Parisiis: 1904), n. 110, nota 1; Schuster, *The Sacramentary* (5 vols., London: Burnes, Oates & Washbourne, Ltd., 1924), I, 146; Smith-Cheetham, *A Dictionary of Christian Antiquities* (2 vols., Hartford: 1180), v. "consecration of churches," n. 3— I, 430.

[38] *Epist. XXII*, n. 1: "Nam cum basilicam dedicassem, multi tamquam uno ore interpretare coeperunt dicentes: 'Sicut Romanam basilicam dedices.' Respondi: 'faciam, si martyrum reliquias invenero.' "—*MPL*, XVI, 1019.

[39] *Ibid.*, n. 2, 13—*MPL*, XVI, 1019, 1023.

Ambrose did not explain in what the ceremonies consisted, but it can be inferred from his sermon that the consecration consisted principally in the solemn transfer of the relics of SS. Agricola and Vitalis. [40] St. Gregory of Tours (circa 538-594) dedicated an oratory in Gaul, consecrating the altar and placing relics in it.[41]

It soon became the custom for every consecrating prelate to place relics, if they were obtainable, in the churches during the time of their consecration. Wherever the practice was not carried out, it was because of the lack of relics. Even though the placing of relics was looked upon as being of great importance, nevertheless there was no legislation requiring it. The deposition of relics in a church, therefore, was not so essential to its consecration that without it the consecration was considered invalid. Pope Vigilius (538-555), in a letter written in 538 to Eutherius, Bishop of Braga, explained that the consecration of a church could take place either with or without the deposition of relics. In the first case the ceremony consisted in placing the relics in the church with the celebration of Mass following; in the latter the only requirement was the celebration of Mass.[42]

The VII Ecumenical Council, the second of Nicaea,held in 787, decreed that all churches which had been consecrated without the relics of martyrs should have relics placed in them with the customary prayers, and that any bishop thenceforth consecrating a church without relics should be deposed from office as one transgressing ecclesiastical traditions.[43] Less than thirty years later, at the Council

[40] "Munera itaque salutis accipite, quae nunc sub altaribus reconduntur. Ea igitur vidua sancta est Iuliana, quae hoc Domino templum paravit atque obtulit, quod hodie dedicamus."—*Exhortatio Virginitatis*, cap. 2, n. 10—*MPL*, XVI, 339.

[41] *De Gloria Confessorum*, cap. 20—*MPL*, LXXI, 842.

[42] *Epist.* I, n. 4—*MPL*, LXIX, 18; *Mansi*, *Sacrorum Conciliorum Nova et Amplissima Collectio* (53 vols. in 59, Paris, Arnhem-Leipzig, 1901-1927), IX, 31-32; Hardouin, *Acta Conciliorum et Epistolae Decretales ac Constitutiones Summorum Pontificum* (12 vols., Parisiis: 1715), II, 1431-1432; Hinschius, *Decretales Pseudo-Isidorianae et Capitula Angilramni* (Lipsiae: 1863), p. 711; cf. also Jaffé, *Regesta Pontificum Romanorum ab condita Ecclesia ad annum post Christum natum MCXCVIII* (ed. 2., 2 vols. in 1, correctam et auctam auspiciis Gulielmi Wattenbach curaverunt S. Loewenfeld, F. Kaltenbrunner, P. Ewald, Lipsiae: 1885-1888), n. 907.

[43] C. 7: "Quotquot ergo venerabilia templa consecrata sunt absque sanctis

of Chelsea (816) in England, it was ordered that the bishop of the diocese should consecrate the church according to the liturgical books, and that the Holy Eucharist should be placed in a receptacle with the other relics and kept in the church; furthermore, if relics could not be obtained, it was sufficient that the Body and Blood of Jesus Christ be preserved.[44]

Between the sixth and the eighth centuries there appeared various liturgical books which contained, among other things, the rite for the dedication of a church. The Gelasian Sacramentary, attributed to Pope St. Gelasius (492-496), gives the liturgical order followed in Gaul from the sixth to the eighth centuries by many churches which desired to conform to the Roman custom.[45] It makes no reference to the ceremony of the deposition of relics, but merely gives the orations which were to be said over the water and wine which was used at the consecration of the altar. It also listed the orations which were used for the consecration of the altar, for the blessing of the linens and for the consecration of the chalice and paten and, finally, the orations which were to be included in the Mass of dedication.[46]

The Gregorian Sacramentary allegedly was compiled under the authority of Pope St. Gregory the Great (590-604). About the year 788 it was sent by Pope Adrian I to Charlemagne. The original

reliquiis martyrum, definimus in eis reliquiarum una cum solita oratione fieri positionem. Et si a praesenti tempore fuerit episcopus absque lipsanis consecrare templum, deponatur, ut ille qui ecclesiasticas traditiones transgreditur." —Mansi, XIII, 751; Hardouin, IV, 491; cf. Schroeder, *Disciplinary Decrees of the General Councils* (St. Louis: Herder, 1937), p. 148.

[44] *Synodus apud Celichtych*, anno 816, c. 2: "Ubi ecclesia aedificatur, a propriae diocesis episcopo sanctificetur: aqua per semetipsum benedicatur, spargatur, et ita per ordinem compleat, sicut in libro ministeriali habetur. Postea Eucharistia quae ab episcopo per idem ministerium consecratur, cum aliis reliquiis condatur in capsula, ac servetur in eadem basilica. Et si alias reliquias intimare non potest, tamen hoc maxime proficere potest, quia corpus et sanguis est Domini nostri Jesu Christi."—Hardouin, IV, 1220; cf. also Duchesne, *Christian Worship*, p. 403.

[45] Cicognani, *Canon Law* (2. ed., Philadelphia: Dolphin Press, 1935), p. 231.

[46] *Sacramentarium Gelasianum*—*MPL*, LXXIV, 1138-1142; Muratori, *Liturgia Romana Vetus* (2 vols., Venetiis: 1748), I, 609-614.

of the Sacramentary was often copied and added to, so that its text describes the liturgy of Pope Adrian rather than that of Pope Gregory's day.[47]

The rite of consecration, as given in the Gregorian Sacramentary, consisted in the following ceremonies: sprinkling the lower and upper portions of the church with water blessed particularly for that purpose; tracing the letters of the Greek and Latin alphabets on the pavement of the church; consecrating the altar by the use of holy oils; depositing the relics of saints in the altars; anointing the walls of the church in twelve places; and, finally, celebrating the Mass of Dedication.[48] It is interesting to note that the ceremonies here described are essentially the same as those in use at the present time.[49]

[47] Cicognani, *loc. cit.*; Van Hove, *Commentarium Lovaniense*, Vol. I, Tom. I, *Prolegomena ad Codicem Iuris Canonici* (Mechliniae: H. Dessain, 1928), n. 139.

[48] Muratori, *op. cit.*, II, 467-489; S. *Gregorii Magni Liber Sacramentorum* —*MPL*, LXXVIII, 152-162.

[49] Cf. *Pontificale Romanum Summorum Pontificum iussu editum a Benedicto XIV et Leone XIII Pontificibus Maximis recognitum et castigatum* (Ratisbonae: 1891), tit. *De ecclesiae dedicatione seu consecratione.*

Chapter II

HISTORICAL DEVELOPMENT FROM THE EARLIEST TIMES UP TO THE DECRETALS OF GREGORY IX

Article I. Desecration of Churches

A. *Destruction*

It was the common practice during the earlier middle ages to consecrate anew the churches which were rebuilt after they had been previously destroyed. The consecration of a church was performed by the bishop, but in Italy the bishops had to obtain permission from the Pope before they could licitly proceed with the ceremony.[1] Thus Pope St. Gregory the Great (590-604) granted Bishop Leontius permission to consecrate a church which had been restored after its destrucion by fire.[2] The *Liber Diurnus Romanorum Pontificum*, a collection of formularies used from the fifth to the eleventh century by the Apostolic Chancery for the execution of documents, contains an example of a formula which was used to grant bishops permission to reconsecrate churches which had been destroyed by fire.[3] Another formula in the same collection indicates that a new dedication was to be given to a church which had been constructed either from the material of the ruins of a church which had collapsed or from entirely different material.[4]

Since it was required that destroyed churches be consecrated after

[1] Gelasius Papa, *ad Episcopos Lucaniae:* "Basilicas noviter institutas, non petitis ex more praeceptionibus, dedicare nemo audeat."—*Epist.* V, cap. 4 (anno 494)—Hardouin, II, 899; c. 6, D.I, *de cons.*

[2] "Basilicam beati Stephani martyris, quam fraternitas vestra incendio asserit concrematam, quam etiam nuper instauratam esse commemorat, facultatem tribuimus dedicandi, in qua etiam reliquiarum sanctuaria ejusdem beati Stephani martyris volumus collocari. Et ideo, frater charissime, ad praedictam te ecclesiam ire necesse est, et tam Ecclesiae quam etiam altaris noviter constructi dedicationem solemniter exhibere."—Lib. VI, epist. 45, *ad Leontium Episcopum*—*MPL*, LXXVII, 832.

[3] De Rozière, *Liber Diurnus ou Recueil des Formules usitées par la Chancellerie Pontificale du Ve au XIe siècle* (Paris: 1869), n. XXVII, p. 53.

[4] *Ibid.*, n. XXVIII, p. 55.

their restoration, it is evident that churches lost their consecration when they were destroyed.

In 538 Pope Vigilius, in response to some questions proposed by Bishop Eutherius of Braga, wrote that it was not sufficient to sprinkle with holy water a church which was destroyed and later rebuilt, but that it was necessary to consecrate it again.[5] He distinguished between churches which contained relics and those which did not. This difference, however, affected the manner in which the churches were to be reconsecrated. Destroyed churches which had no relics were to be reconsecrated by offering the sacrifice of the Mass, whereas destroyed churches which contained relics were to be reconsecrated by replacing the relics, if they had been previously removed, and by offering the sacrifice of the Mass. These were the only ceremonies known at the time of Pope Vigilius. More elaborate ceremonies were added in the eighth century.

The letter of Pope Vigilius was incorporated into the *Pseudo-Isidorian Collection* (circa 847)[6] and later into the *Decretum* (circa 1012) of Burchard of Worms[7] and the *Decretum* (circa 1090-1095) and *Panormia* (circa 1095) of Ivo, Bishop of Chartres,[8] and finally into the *Decretum* of Gratian (1140).[9]

The *Excerpts* of Egbert (747), Archbishop of York, contain this regulation concerning the walls of a church: "*si parietes mutantur*

[5] "De fabrica vero cuiuslibet ecclesiae instuaranda, si diruta fuerit, et si in eo loco consecrationis solemnitas debeat iterari, in quo sanctuaria non fuerint, nihil judicamus officere, si per eam minime aqua benedicta jactetur: quia consecrationem cuiuslibet ecclesiàe, in qua Spiritus sancti ara non ponitur, celebritatem tantum scimus esse missarum. Et ideo, si qua sanctorum basilica a fundamentis etiam fuerit innovata sine altaris motione, sine aliqua dubitatione, cum in ea missarum fuerit celebrata solemnitas, totius sanctificatio consecrationis implebitur. Si vero sanctuaria qua habebat, ablata sunt, rursus eorum repositione, et missarum solemnitate, reverentiam sanctificationis accipiet."—*Epist. I*, c. 4—*MPL*, LXIX, 18; Hardouin, II, 1431; Mansi, IX, 31-32; Jaffé, *Regesta Pontificum Romanorum ab condita Ecclesia ad annum post Christum natum MCXCVIII*, n. 907.

[6] Hinschius, *Decretales Pseudo-Isidorianae et Capitula Angilramni*, p. 711.

[7] Lib. III, cap. 62—*MPL*, CXL, 686.

[8] *Decretum*, pars III, cap. 25—*MPL*, CLXI, 204; *Panormia*, lib. II, cap. 14—*MPL*, CLXI, 1085.

[9] C. 24, D.I, *de cons.*

. . . *salibus tantum [ecclesia] exorcizetur.*" [10] This decree was incorporated in the *Decretum* of Gratian.[11] Rufinus († circa 1190) and Stephen of Tournai (Stephanus Tornacensis, 1135-1203), contemporaries of Gratian, explained that this decree did not contemplate the total collapse of the walls of a church, but only of a small part thereof, otherwise this decree would have been contrary to the decree of Pope Vigilius, which spoke of the reconsecration of a church which had been totally destroyed.[12] Hence the collapse of a small portion of the walls of a church did not cause the church to be desecrated, and it was not necessary to reconsecrate such a church. The only requirement was that the destroyed portion be sprinkled with holy water after the wall was repaired.[13]

The *Decretum* of Gratian contained a decree which forbade the reconsecration of churches that had already been consecrated to God, unless they had been consumed by fire.[14] According to the *glossa*

[10] C. 139, *Excerptiones Egberti*—*MPL*, LXXXIX, 396; Hardouin, III, 1974; Mansi, XII, 426; Ivo of Chartres, *Decretum*, pars III, cap. 13—*MPL*, CLXI, 202; *Panormia*, lib. II, cap. 20—*MPL*, CLXI, 1087; Burchard, *Decretum*, lib. III, cap. 11—*MPL*, CXL, 675.

[11] C. 19, D.I, *de cons.*

[12] "*Si parietes mutantur*—non utique a fundamentis, sed super edificatione; vel si a fundamentis, non tamen per totum, sed per aliquam partem . . . alioquin contrarium esset . . . capitula (c. 24, D.I, *de cons.*)"—Singer, *Die Summa Decretorum des Magister Rufinus* (Paderborn: 1902), p. 544; J. Schulte, *Die Summa des Stephanus Tornacensis uber das Decretum Gratiani* (Giessen: 1891), p. 266.

[13] "*Salibus exorcizetur*, i.e., aqua cum sale exorcizata aspergatur."—Rufinus, *Summa Decretorum*, ed. Singer, p. 544; Stephanus Tornacenis, *Summa*, ed. J. Schulte, p. 266.

[14] The full text of this decree is as follows: "Ecclesiis semel Deo consecratis non debet iterum consecratio adhiberi, nisi aut ab igne exustae, aut sanguinis effusione, aut cujuscumque semine pollutae fuerint." — C. 3, D.LXVIII. This decree is repeated in c. 20, D. I, *de cons.* The origin of this decree is not known. Gratian falsely attributed it to the Council of Nicaea, but no such legislation is found in either the first or the second council held in that city. It was very probably written by some person not too far removed from the time of Gratian and attributed to the Council of Nicaea in order that it would more readily gain widespread attention and approval. —Cf. Berardi, *Gratiani Canones Genuini ab Apocryphis Discreti* (4 vols., Venetiis: 1777), I, 76. Richter-Friedberg admit that this decree could not be

on this decree there were two possible means by which a church could become desecrated as the result of a fire. The first was the destruction of a church to such an extent that the walls collapsed. The other was the destruction of the plaster of the walls (*decrustatio*), the walls themselves remaining standing. It is clear from what has already been said that in the first instance the desecration of a church resulted from its destruction. In the second case a church was desecrated by the falling of the plaster from the walls. The reason for this is that in the ceremony of the consecration of a church the walls were anointed with chrism, and since the chrism was applied to the surface of the walls, or to the plaster, it was considered that the consecration adhered to the surface of the walls. Thus, whenever the plaster was removed, the consecration was lost.[15]

B. *Removal of the Altar*

The removal of the altar from the church was another means by which a church became desecrated during this period. The *Excerpts* of Egbert (747) contain the regulation for this manner of desecration: "*si motum fuerit altare, denuo consecretur ecclesia.*" [16] This decree was incorporated into the *Decretum* of Burchard of Worms,[17] the *Decretum* and *Panormia* of Ivo of Chartres[18] and the *Decretum* of Gratian.[19] All of these collections falsely attribute the decree to Pope Hyginus (circa 136-140). It is hardly possible that

found in any of the collections of law which were at their disposal.—*Corpus Iuris Canonici* (ed Lipsiensis II, 2 vols., Lipsiae: 1879-1881—editio anastatice repetita, Lipsiae: Tauchnitz, 1928), I, 254, ad D. LXVIII, nota 28.

15 For the rite of consecration of churches used in the eighth century cf. *Liber Sacramentorum* in Muratori, *Liturgia Romana Vetus*, II, 467-489; also *MPL*, LXXVIII, 152-162; " . . . *exusta*—pro majori parte, scil. ita comburitur ecclesia quod destruatur vel decrustatur interius et exterius, tunc execratur. Consecratio enim ecclesiae maxime consistit in unctione exteriori, et coniunctione et dispositione lapidum."—*glossa* in c. 20, D. I, *de cons.*

16 C. 139, *Excerptiones Egberti*—*MPL*, LXXXIX, 396; Hardouin, III, 1974; Mansi, XII, 426.

17 Lib. III, cap. 11—*MPL*, CXL, 675.

18 *Decretum*, pars III, cap. 13—*MPL*, CLXI, 202; *Panormia*, lib. II, cap. 20—*MPL*, CLXI, 1087.

19 C. 19, D. I, *de cons.*

Pope Hyginus issued any decree concerning the consecration of churches, since no ceremony of consecration was used during the second century. Thus there could not be any possibility of the reconsecration of churches at such an early date.[20]

The *Excerpts* of Egbert attribute the decree to Pope Vigilius (538-555), but there is no mention of any such decree in any of his works. Since the origin of the decree is uncertain, it can be safely said that the practice of reconsecrating churches desecrated by the removal of the altar was in use at least from the middle of the eighth century until the middle of the twelfth century, that is, until the time of Gratian inclusively.

Ivo, Bishop of Chartres (1091-1115), in a letter written probably before the compilation of his *Decretum* and *Panormia,* said that he did not know of any law requiring the reconsecration of an altar which had been moved, but he was fully aware of a law requiring the reconsecration of a church, if the altar had been removed.[21] St. Anselm, Archbishop of Canterbury (1093-1109), wrote that he had discussed the question of the reconsecration of churches with Pope Urban II (1088-1099) and some bishops. All agreed that when the principal altar was removed or destroyed it was necessary to consecrate the church again, and care should be taken that the consecration of an altar should accompany the consecration of a church. The reason for this, as given by him, lies in the fact that the altar does not exist because of the church, but the church exists because of the altar, and it seems that a building can no longer be considered a church when its altar is destroyed.[22]

[20] Cf. Berardi, *Gratiani Canones Genuini ab Apocryphis Discreti,* II, 62.

[21] "De motione altaris . . . utrum iteranda sit consecratio, vel non iteranda, nihil scriptum in antiquis regulis reperi. In collectionibus autem Burchardi Wormacensis episcopi . . . ita scriptum reperitur: Altare si motum fuerit, ecclesia denuo consecretur."—*Epist. LXXX (Guilelmo, Fiscanensis monasterii abbati)—MPL,* CLXII, 101; cf. also *Epist. LXXII*—MPL, CLXII, 92.

[22] "De his [de moto altari] cum domino papa Urbano locutus sum, assistentibus quibusdam episcopis. . . . In his autem omnes concordant, quod violato principali, tota ecclesia cum altari iterum consecranda est, nec ecclesia consecranda est sine consecratione altaris, aut principalis, aut alicujus alterius in eadem ecclesia. . . . Altare non fit propter ecclesiam sed ecclesia propter altare; et ideo, violato principali altari, jam non videtur esse ecclesia."—

The question of the desecration of a church as a consequence of the removal or the destruction of its altar arose again during the pontificate of Alexander III (1159-1181). The practice which had been in use up to this time was completely changed. The Pope was asked whether or not a church should be reconsecrated if its altar was moved, or if the table of the altar was broken or if it was removed from its support. The response of the Pope was that it was not necessary to consecrate the church again even though the canons seemed to indicate otherwise.[23]

C. *Homicide and the Shedding of Blood*

The History of the Franks, written by St. Gregory, Bishop of Tours (573-594), gives an account of a certain Godegisilus who, fleeing from his attackers, sought refuge in a church where the bishop tried to protect him. Upon the refusal of the bishop to deliver him to the pursuers, they gained access to the roof and, removing the tiles, hurled them into the church, killing Godegisilus and three servants. The bishop was greatly saddened not only because he could not protect the man but also because the church was polluted with human blood.[24] It is to be noted that the writer used the expression *polluted,* but did not explain the extent of the meaning of the word. There was no conciliar legislation or any papal

Opera Omnia, lib. III, *Epist.* CLIX *(ad Willelmum abbatem)—MPL,* CLIX, 194-195.

[23] "Ad haec si altare motum fuerit, lapis ille solummodo supra positus, qui sigillum continet confractus, aut etiam diminutus exstiterit, debet denuo consecrari. Propter hoc vero, nequaquam reitérare suam consecrationem ecclesiam consuevit, licet id quidem canones innuere videantur."—Augustinus, *Antiquae decretalium collectiones commentariis et emendationibus illustrate* (Parisiis: 1621), Comp. II, c. un. *de consecratione ecclesiae vel altaris,* V, 20 (hereafter this work will be referred to as *Antiquae decretalium collectiones*); Jaffé, *Regesta Pontificum Romanorum,* n. 14204. This decretal was later included in the Decretals of Gregory IX, published in 1234, which had the force of universal law up to the publication of the present Code. Cf. c. 1, X, *de consecratione ecclesiae vel altaris,* III, 40.

[24] "Multum ex hoc episcopus dolens, quod eum non solum defensare non potuit, verum etiam locum in quo orare consueverat, et in quo sanctorum pignora aggregata fuerant, sanguine humano pollui vidit."—*Historia Francorum,* lib. IX, n. 12—*MPL,* LXII, 491.

decree at this early date concerning the effects upon a church that the shedding of blood produced. The first extant legislation, the origin of which is unknown, is found in the *Decretum* of Gratian, where it is falsely ascribed to the Council of Nicaea.[25] The decree orders: "*Ecclesiis semel Deo consecratis non debet iterum consecratio adhiberi, nisi . . . sanguinis effusione . . . pollutae fuerint.*"[26] This decree used the word *pollutae*, which undoubtedly has the meaning of desecration, or of the loss of consecration, for reconsecration was required when blood was shed in the church. Since the origin of this decree is unknown, it may be assumed that the practice of reconsecrating churches polluted by bloodshed dated back to the time of St. Gregory of Tours.

The killing of an animal in a church and the subsequent flowing of blood from its body did not desecrate a church. Desecration resulted from the shedding of human blood caused, for example, by homicide or the infliction of a wound.[27]

The crime of homicide committed in a church, whether or not it was accompanied with bloodshed, caused the church to lose its consecration. The law stated simply that if a church was violated through homicide, it was to be cleansed very carefully and consecrated again. The decree, falsely attributed to Pope Vigilius, is found in the collection of laws compiled by Egbert, Archbishop of York, in 747.[28] It was later embodied in the canonical collections of the eleventh and twelfth centuries and in these it was falsely accredited to Pope Hyginus (circa 136-140).[29]

[25] Cf. Berardi, *Gratiani Canones Genuini ab Apocryphis Discreti*, I, p. 76; Richter-Friedberg, *Corpus Iuris Canonici*, I, 254, nota 28 ad D.LXVIII.

[26] C. 20, D. I, *de cons.*; c. 3, D.LXVIII.

[27] Cf. Stephanus Tornacensis, *Summa*, ad c. 3, D.LXVIII et c. 20, D.I, *de cons.*—ed. J. Schulte, pp. 94, 266; Rufinus, *Summa Decretorum*, ad c. 20, D.I, *de cons.*—ed. Singer, p. 544.

[28] "Si homicidio . . . ecclesia violata fuerit, diligentissime expurgetur et denuo consecretur."—C. 139, *Excerptiones Egberti*—*MPL*, LXXXIX, 396; Mansi, XII, 426; Hardouin, III, 1974.

[29] Burchard, *Decretum*, lib. III, cap. 12—*MPL*, CXL, 675; Ivo, *Decretum*, pars III, cap. 14—*MPL*, CLXI, 202; Ivo, *Panormia*, lib. II, cap. 21—*MPL*, CLXI, 1087; Gratian, c. 19, D.I, *de cons.*

D. *Effusio Seminis*

The *Excerpts* of Egbert (747), Archbishop of York, contain this decree: "*Si . . . adulterio ecclesia fuerit violata, diligentissime expurgetur, et denuo consecretur.*"[30] Since adultery is mentioned explicitly, it seems that all other carnal acts committed in a church did not cause it to lose its consecration. This decree was incorporated into the *Decretum* of Gratian,[31] which also contains another decree in which it seems to be indicated that all carnal acts committed in a church caused it to lose its consecration: "*Ecclesiis semel Deo consecratis non debet iterum consecratio adhiberi nisi . . . cujuscumque semine pollutae fuerint.*"[32] It is very improbable that an act which of itself was not sinful caused a church to become desecrated. This opinion was substantiated by the *glossa*, where it is said that a church should not be reconsecrated in consequence of an *effusio seminis* which occurred during sleep or in an act of marital relationship between husband and wife, but the *effusio seminis* involved the desecration of a church when it occurred as an act of fornication or adultery.[33]

Article 2. Canonical Effects of the Burial of Infidels in a Church

The burial of an infidel in a church was strictly prohibited at all times. This prohibition was based upon the principle given by Pope Leo the Great (440-461): "*Nos autem quibus viventibus non communicavimus, mortuis communicare non possumus.*"[34] However, it happened occasionally, contrary to the discipline of the times, that a pagan was buried in a church. The Penitential attributed

[30] C. 139—MPL, LXXXIX, 396; Mansi, XII, 426; Hardouin, III, 1974. This decree is also contained in Burchard, *Decretum*, lib. III, cap. 12—MPL. CXL, 675; Ivo, *Decretum*, pars III, cap. 14—MPL. CLXI, 202; Ivo, *Panormia*, lib. II, cap. 21—MPL, CLXI, 1087.

[31] C. 19, D.I, *de cons.*

[32] C. 20, D.I, *de cons.*; c. 3, D.LXVIII. The origin of this decree is not known; cf. Berardi, *Gratiani Canones Genuini ab Apocryphis Discreti*, I, p. 76; Richter-Friedberg, *Corpus Iuris Canonici*, I, 254, nota 28 ad D.LXVIII.

[33] Cf. *glossa* ad c. 20, D.I, *de cons.*, v. "semine."

[34] *Epist.* CLVII *(ad Rusticum Narbonensi episcopum)*—MPL, LIV, 1026; Jaffé, *Regesta Pontificum Romanorum*, n. 320.

to Archbishop Theodore of Canterbury, compiled about 673, contains the following regulation on the subject:

> "In ecclesia ubi mortuorum cadavera infidelium sepeliuntur, sacrificare non licet; sed si apta videtur ad consecrandam, inde evulsa, et rasis vel lotis lignis ejus reaedificetur. Si haec consecrata prius fuit, missas in ea celebrare licet si religiosi ibi sepulti sunt. Si vero paganus, sic mundare et jactare foras melius est."[35]

From the wording of this text it is clear that the burial of a pagan in a consecrated church did not cause the church to lose its consecration. The effect produced by the burial of a pagan in a consecrated church was the prohibition to celebrate Mass in the church until the body was removed and the church was cleansed. The burial of a pagan in a church was an indication of grave disrespect for the sanctity of the sacred building, but its sanctity was not lost. It was considered as having been marred or blemished. The celebration of Mass was prohibited as long as the blemish continued to exist. The removal of the body from the church and the subsequent purification were the means by which the blemish was removed and by which the pristine sanctity was restored to the church. There is no doubt, then, that the burial of a pagan in a consecrated church caused the church to become violated or polluted, although this terminology was not used in the *Penitential of Theodore*.

The spurious collection of Benedict the Levite,[36] compiled between 847 and 857, contains canon 1 of the *Penitential of Theodore*, but in a mutilated form. The compiler substituted the word *fideles* in place of *religiosi*, and totally omitted the last sentence of the canon.[37] Later, the canon was incorporated in its mutilated form into the

[35] *Theodori Poenitentiale*, c.1—*MPL*, XCIX, 927.

[36] *Capitularium Karoli Magni et Ludovici Pii*, lib. V, c. 111—Mansi, XVII B, 843.

[37] Seckel asserts that canon 111 of the fifth book of Benedict the Levite's work is taken from Theodore's *Penitential*; cf. art. "*Studien zu Benedictus Levita*," pp. 61-179 in *Neues Archiv der Gesellschaft für ältere Deutsche Geschichtskunde*, XXXI (1905), especially p. 71.

[38] *Decretum*, lib. III, cap. 38—*MPL*, CXL, 679.

collections of Burchard of Worms,[38] Ivo of Chartres[39] and Gratian.[40] In all of these it was falsely attributed to a Council of Cologne.[41] With the exception of the work of Benedict the Levite, all of the other collections contain another canon which is nothing more than a condensation of the above quoted canon from Theodore's *Penitential*.[42] Gratian, whose work was more systematic and more widely used than any other previous collection, placed these two mutilated canons one after the other so that it could be more readily understood how a church became violated, what were the effects of such a violation, and what was required to remove the blemish inflicted upon the sanctity of the church through its violation.[43]

[39] *Decretum*, *par III*, *cap*. 43—*MPL*, CLXI, 207; *Panormia*, lib. II, cap. 23 and 24—*MPL*, CLXI, 1088.

[40] C. 28, D. I, *de cons*.

[41] Cf. Berardi, *Gratiani Canones Genuini ab Apocryphis Discreti*, I, p. 408; Richter-Friedberg, *Corpus Iuris Canonici*, I, 1301, nota 290, ad D.I, *de cons*.

[42] "Ecclesiam, ubi paganus sepultus est, non liceat consecrari, neque missas in ea celebrari, sed iactare foras, et mundari oportet."—c. 27, D.I, *de cons*.; Burchard, *Decretum*, lib. III, cap. 13—*MPL*, CXL, 676; Ivo, *Decretum*, pars III, cap. 15—*MPL*, CLXI, 202; Ivo, *Panormia*, lib. II, cap. 22—*MPL*, CLXI, 1088. All of these collections falsely ascribe the canon to a Council of Orleans, but it is not contained in the decrees issued at any of the councils held there; cf. Berardi, *op. cit*., I, 279, and Richter-Friedberg, *op. cit*., I, 1301, nota 283 ad D.I, *de cons*., both of whom assert that the canon is taken from the *Penitential of Theodore*.

[43] Cc. 27 and 28, D.I, *de cons*.

Chapter III

HISTORICAL DEVELOPMENT FROM THE DECRETALS OF GREGORY IX UP TO THE CODE

Article 1. Desecration of Churches

With the promulgation of the Decretals of Gregory IX, in 1234, the legislation concerning the desecration of churches underwent a great change. Prior to this time a church lost its consecration by the destruction of the church, the removal or destruction of the altar, the shedding of human blood, the crime of homicide and the inherently sinful *effusio seminis*. During the period now under discussion the desecration of a church resulted simply from its total destruction, from the destruction of the major part of its walls and from its conversion to profane uses.

A. *Total Destruction*

In the year 1212 the following problem was presented to Pope Innocent III. The supporting beams of the roof of a church were destroyed by a fire which caused the roof to collapse. The walls of the church, however, were not damaged. It was asked whether or not the church should be consecrated again after the necessary repairs were made. The Pope replied that no consecration was necessary, provided the walls of the church remained intact.[1] The consecration of a church consisted in anointing with chrism the walls, and not the roof, of the church. Hence, as long as the walls remained intact it was not necessary to consecrate the church again.[2] It follows, then, that a church became desecrated when its walls had been totally destroyed. This was the universal opinion of auth-

[1] "Ligneis aedificiis ecclesiae vestrae casu quodam igne consumptis, parietibus tamen illaesis . . . respondendum quod, cum parietes in sua integritate permanserint . . . ob causam praedictam nec ecclesia . . . debet denuo consecrari."—C. 6, X, *de consecratione ecclesiae vel altaris*, III, 40. This letter was previously published in the earlier collection of the decretals, cf. Augustinus, *Antiquae Decretalium Collectiones*, Compilatio IV, c. un. *de cons. eccl. vel altaris*, III, 14.

[2] *Glossa* in c. 6, X, *de consecratione ecclesiae vel altaris*, III, 40, v. "parietibus."

ors.[3] The Sacred Congregation of Rites declared that a church which was built upon the site of a former church was to be consecrated,[4] because the consecration was lost by the destruction of the former church. Even though a destroyed church was rebuilt from the same material that had been used in its original construction, it was necessary to consecrate the church again, because the restored building did not retain the consecration of the former building, nor could it be said to be the same building; it was considered to be an entirely new building.[5]

[3] Barbosa, *Ius Ecclesiasticum Universum*, lib. II, cap. 2, n. 46; Pirhing, *Ius Canonicum Nova Methodo Explicatum* (5 vols. in 4, Dilingae: 1674-1678), lib. III, tit. 40, n. 8; Benedictus XIV, ep. *Ex tuis precibus*, 16 nov. 1748, § 1—*Fontes*, n. 393; allocut. *Postquam*, 30 sept. 1750, § 1—*Fontes*, n. 408; ep. *Iam inde*, 12 maii 1756, §§ 7-9—*Fontes*, n. 440; Gonzalez-Tellez, *Commentaria Perpetua in . . . Quinque Libros Decretalium Gregorii IX* (5 vols. in 4, Venetiis: 1699), lib. III, tit. 40, cap. 7, n. 4; Reiffenstuel, *Ius Canonicum Universum* (5 vols. in 7, Parisiis: 1864-1882), lib. III, tit. 40, n. 11; Schmalzgrueber, *Ius Ecclesiasticum Universum*, lib. III, tit. 40, n. 23; Gasparri, *De Ssma. Eucharistia*, I, n. 181; Wernz, *Ius Decretalium*, III, n. 441; Hinschius, *Das Kirchenrecht der Katholiken und Protestanten in Deutschland* (6 vols., Berlin: 1869-1897. Vols. I-IV, *System des katholischen Kirchenrechts*, Berlin: 1869-1888), IV, 331 (henceforth this work will be referred to as *System des katholischen Kirchenrechts)*; Scherer, *Handbuch des Kirchenrechts* (2 vols., Graz und Leipzig: 1886-1898), II, p. 631; Santi, *Praelectiones Iuris Canonici* (4 vols. in 2, Ratisbonae: 1886), lib. III, tit. 40, n. 5; Bargilliat, *Praelectiones Iuris Canonici* (25. ed., 2 vols., Parisiis: 1909), n. 1278; Many, *De Locis Sacris*, n. 26.

[4] *Caesaraugustana*, 31 aug. 1872, ad I—*Decreta Authentica Congregationis Sacrorum Rituum ex Actis eiusdem collecta eiusque auctoritate promulgata sub auspiciis SS.. D. N. Leonis Papae XIII* (6 vols., Romae: 1898-1927), n. 3269 (hereafter this work will be referred to as *Decr. Auth.)*; Gardellini, *Decreta Authentica Congregationis Sacrorum Rituum . . .* (3. ed., 4 vols. cum appendicibus, Romae: 1856-1887), n. 5508 (hereafter cited as Gardellini, *Decr. Auth.*).

[5] Cf. Barbosa, *Pastoralis Solicitudinis sive De Officio et Potestate Episcopi Tripartita Descriptio* (Lugduni: 1656), pars II, allegatio 27, n. 15 (hereafter this work shall be referred to as *De Officio et Potestate Episcopi)*; Panormitanus (Nicholaus de Tudeschis), *Commentaria in Quinque Libros Decretalium* (5 vols. in 7, Venetiis: 1588), in c. 4 X, *de cons. eccl. vel altaris*, III, 40, n. 8; Reiffenstuel, *Ius Canonicum Universum*, lib. III, tit. 40, n. 11; Schmalzgrueber, *Ius Ecclesiasticum Universum*, lib. III, tit. 40, n. 25; Ferraris, *Prompta Bibliotheca, Canonica, Juridica, Moralis, Theologica, Necnon Asce-*

B. *Destruction of the Major Part of the Walls*

The letter of Pope Innocent III, referred to in the preceeding article, insisted that a church did not lose its consecration provided the walls remained intact. In the case presented to the Pope, the supporting beams of the roof were consumed by fire. Undoubtedly the walls suffered some slight damage at the places where the beams were upheld by the walls. A slight damage, however, was not considered serious enough to cause the desecration of a church. All authors, using the Pope's letter as a basis for their contention, were in agreement that a church lost its consecration solely by the destruction of the major part of the walls. In 1875 the restoration of a church was completed from the ruins of an old church. Prior to the restoration it was found that one entire wall and the apse of the church had been destroyed. In the process of restoration the deficient walls were rebuilt. Upon presentation of the aforesaid facts to the Sacred Congregation of Rites it was declared by the Congregation that the church had to be consecrated again.[6]

It was long the common opinion of the canonists that a church also lost its consecration when the plaster of the walls was removed or destroyed either totally or to a major degree. The reason for their contention was based upon the fact that the surface of the wall was anointed with chrism when the church was consecrated. Thus the consecration was considered lost with the destruction of the plaster.[7] It was necessary to abandon this opinion in 1882 when the Sacred Congregation of Rites declared that a church did not lose its consecration when the plaster was entirely removed for the purpose of covering the walls with marble. The only requirement

tica, Polemica, Rubricistica, Historica (ed. Migne, 8 vols., Parisiis: 1860-1863), v. "ecclesia," art. 4, n. 19 (hereafter referred to as *Prompta Bibliotheca).*

[6] *Aretina,* 4 sept. 1875, ad II—*Decr. Auth.,* n. 3372; Gardellini, *Decr. Auth.,* n. 5632.

[7] Panormitanus, in c. 4, X, *de consecratione ecclesiae vel altaris,* III, 40, n. 7; Pirhing, *Ius Canonicum,* lib. III, tit. 40, n. 8; Reiffenstuel, *Ius Canonicum Universum,* lib. III, tit. 40, n. 13; Barbosa, *Ius Ecclesiasticum Universum,* lib. II, cap. 2, n. 46; Schmalzgrueber, *Ius Ecclesiasticum Universum,* lib. III, tit. 40, n. 23; Benedictus XIV, ep. "*Iam inde,*" 12 maii 1756, § 7—*Fontes* n. 440.

made by the Sacred Congregation was that the twelve crosses, which were removed with the plaster, should be painted or engraved on the walls as evidence that the church has been previously consecrated.[8] A similar decision was given again in 1894.[9]

These decisions did not have the force of a general law, however, since they were replies given to questions proposed from particular localities. In 1896 Pope Leo XIII approved a general decree of the Sacred Congregation of Rites on the same question, whereby the ruling contained in the two earlier decisions became the general law of the church.[10] From these decisions it is apparent that the consecration of a church adheres to the entire wall of the church and not merely to the places which are anointed with chrism.

A church did not lose its consecration if only a small part of the walls was destroyed. When the destroyed portion was rebuilt, it was not necessary to consecrate the church again, for the newly built part automatically became consecrated by its addition to that part of the church which retained its consecration.[11] This opinion was based upon a decretal of Innocent III wherein he stated that a small amount of oil could be added to consecrated oil and the entire mixture would be considered consecrated.[12]

Another basis for the opinion was the legal rule enunciated by Pope Boniface VIII (1294-1303): "That which is the accessory ought to follow the condition of the principal."[13] The Sacred Con-

[8] *Senien. et Modrussen.*, 4 maii 1882—*Decr. Auth.*, n. 3545; Gardellini, *Decr. Auth.*, n. 5840; *Le Canoniste Contemporain*, XVIII (1895), 239.

[9] *Tridentina*, 11 ian. 1894—ASS, XXVII (1894-95), 439; *American Ecclesiastical Review*, XII (1895), 344.

[10] *Decretum*, 19 maii 1896, dubium II (approbatum 8 iunii 1896 a Papa Leone XIII)—*Decr. Auth.*, n. 3907; *Coll. S. C. de Prop. Fide* (ed. 1907), n. 1932; cf. also S.R.C. in *Nicoteren. et Tropien.*, 9 aug. 1897 ad I—*Decr. Auth.*, n. 3962; *Le Canoniste Contemporain*, XX (1897), 710.

[11] Pirhing, *Ius Ecclesiasticum*, lib. III, tit. 40, n. 8; Barbosa, *De Officio et Potestate Episcopi*, pars II, alleg. 27, n. 19; Reiffenstuel, *Ius Canonicum Ecclesiasticum*, lib. III, tit. 40, n. 12.

[12] C. 3, X, *de consecratione ecclesiae vel altaris*, III, 40.

[13] "Accessorium naturam sequi congruit principalis"—Reg. 42, R. J., in VI°. Cicognani, *Canon Law* (English translation by O'Hara and Brennan), p. 794.

gregation of Rites did not require the reconsecration of a church when the destroyed part of the wall amounted to one-twelfth of the total wall area.[14] In another case the entire front wall of a church, consisting of one-sixth of the total wall area, was torn down and rebuilt. The part which was torn down contained two of the twelve crosses which designated the places where the walls had been anointed. Still the Sacred Congregation declared that the church did not have to be reconsecrated.[15]

In like manner, if the walls of a church were rebuilt at various intervals, so that at no one time did the destroyed portion consist of the major part of the walls, the church did not have to be reconsecrated, even though eventually the entire church was rebuilt.[16] The Sacred Congregation of Rites declared that a church did not have to be reconsecrated when additions to the church were made successively and at diverse times, during which the walls of the old church were completely destroyed and removed.[17]

With regard to churches which were merely blessed there were two distinct opinions among the authors concerning their desecration or loss of blessing. Some authors held that a blessed church did not become desecrated by the destruction of its walls either in whole or in a major part. They argued that the blessing adhered to the floor (*pavimento*) of the church and not to the walls. Hence the destruction of the walls did not cause the church to lose its blessing, unless the floor was also destroyed.[18] A blessed church was

[14] *Marianopolitana*, 20 feb. 1874—*Decr. Auth.*, n. 3326; Gardellini, *Decr. Auth.*, n. 5578; *Coll. S. C. de Prop Fide* (ed. 1893), n. 1583; *Coll. S. C. de Prop. Fide* (ed. 1907), n. 1411.

[15] *Marianopolitana*, 11 mar. 1871—*Decr. Auth.*, n. 3240; *Coll. S.C. de Prop. Fide* (ed. 1907), n. 1367.

[16] Barbosa, *De Officio et Potestate Episcopi*, pars II, alleg. 27, n. 19; Pirhing, *Ius Canonicum*, lib. III, tit. 40, n. 9; Schmalzgrueber, *Ius Ecclesiasticum Universum*, lib. III, tit. 40, n. 28; Gasparri, *De Ssma. Eucharistia*, n. 181; Many, *De Locis Sacris*, n. 27, 4°.

[17] *Caesaraugustana*, 31 aug. 1872, ad II—*Decr. Auth.*, n. 3269; Gardellini, *Decr. Auth.*, n. 5508.

[18] Schmalzgrueber, *Ius Ecclesiasticum Universum*, lib. III, tit. 40, n. 16; Suarez, *Opera Omnia* (26 vols., Parisiis: 1856-1866), tract. *De Eucharistia* (Vol. XXI), Disp. LXXXI, sect. 4, n. 7; A. J. Schulte, *Benedicenda* (New York, Cincinnati, Chicago: 1907), p. 87: footnote n. 7.

considered desecrated when it was destroyed by the authority of a legitimate superior and there was no hope of its being rebuilt.[19]

Another group of authors held that a blessed church became desecrated in the same manner as a consecrated church, namely, by total destruction, or also by the destruction of the major part of the walls.[20] They based their contention upon the Roman Ritual, which prescribed that, when a church is blessed, holy water should be sprinkled upon the upper and lower parts of the walls both outside and inside the church.[21] Hence the blessing adhered to the walls, and when they were destroyed the blessing also was lost. This second opinion was given a full legal foundation with the promulgation of the Code.[22]

C. *Reduction to Secular Status and Purpose*

Prior to the Council of Trent (1545-1563) none of the churches, even if they had been destroyed or when they had fallen into ruins, could ever be converted to profane or secular uses. Destroyed churches and the material from which they were constructed could not be used for any other than religious purposes. The material of a former church was to be used in the construction of a new church. The prohibition against the use of such buildings for profane purposes was based upon the principle of Boniface VIII: "Things which are dedicated to God should not be transferred to human (i. e., secular) uses."[23]

The Council of Trent granted bishops the power to convert churches to secular but not sordid uses, provided that the churches had fallen into ruins and it was impossible to raise sufficient funds for the restoration of the churches. When these two conditions were verified, it was then permitted to transfer all of the obligations

[19] Schmalzgrueber, *loc. cit.*; A. J. Schulte, *loc. cit.*

[20] Wernz, *Ius Decretalium*, III, n. 441; Gasparri, *De Ssma. Eucharistia*, n. 183; Many, *De Locis Sacris*, n. 28.

[21] *Rituale Romanum* (ed. 1911), tit. VIII, cap. 27, *Ritus benedicendi novam Ecclesiam*, nn. 3, 11.

[22] Can. 1170.

[23] Reg. 51, R. J., in VI°: "Semel Deo dicatum, non est ad usus humanos ulterius transferendum."

of the former church, along with whatever emoluments they possessed, to the mother church, or to a neighboring church, where an altar or chapel was to be erected under the same title as the former church, and a cross was to be erected upon the site of the former church.[24] By virtue of this decree of the Tridentine Council it was permitted to demolish the church entirely and sell the material, the proceeds being used for the erection of an altar or chapel in the church to which the obligations and emoluments of the former church were transferred.[25]

The Sacred Congregation of the Council on several occasions insisted that the decrees of the Council of Trent be observed in the reduction of churches to a secular status and purpose.[26] It insisted that a bishop could not thus reduce a church and transfer its obligations to another church, unless the former church was in ruins and could not be repaired because of poverty.[27]

[24] Sess. XXI, *de ref.*, c. 7: ". . . episcopi, etiam tanquam apostolicae sedis delegati, transferre possint beneficia simplicia . . . ex ecclesiis, quae vetustate vel alias collapsae sint, et ob eorum inopiam nequeunt restaurari . . . in matrices aut alias ecclesias locorum eorundem seu viciniorum arbitrio suo; atque in eisdem ecclesiis erigant altaria vel capellas sub eisdem invocationibus, vel in iam erecta altaria vel capellas transferant cum omnibus emolumentis et oneribus prioribus ecclesiis impositis. Parochiales vero ecclesias . . . ita collapsas refici et instaurari procurent ex fructibus et proventibus quibuscunque, da easdem ecclesias quomodocunque pertinentibus. Qui si non fuerint sufficientes, omnes patronos et alios, qui fructus aliquos ex dictis ecclesiis provenientes percipiunt, aut, in illorum defectum, parochianos omnibus remediis opportunis ad praedicta cogant, quacunque appellatione, exemptione et contradictione remota. Quod si nimia egestate omnes laborent, ad matrices seu viciniores ecclesias transferantur, cum facultate tam dictas parochiales quam alias ecclesias dirutas in profanos usus non sordidos, erecta tamen ibi cruce, convertendi."

[25] Cf. S.C. Ep. et Reg., *Castellaneten.*, 13 iun. 1589—*Fontes*, n. 1426.

[26] Cf. S.C.C. *Thelesina*, 13 sept. 1631—*Fontes*, n. 2537; Pallottini, *Collectio omnium Conclusionum et Resolutionum Quae in causis propositis apud Sacram Congregationem Cardinalium S. Concilii Tridentini interpretum Prodierunt ab ejus institutione anno MDLXIV ad MDCCCLX, distinctis titulis alphabetico ordine per materias digestas* (17 vols., Romae: 1868-1895), v. "ecclesia in genere," § II, n. 6 (hereafter this work shall be referred to as Pallottini); *Neapolitana*, 13 ian. 1646—*Fontes*, n. 2663.

[27] S.C.C. in *Andrien., 14 mar. 1637*—*Fontes*, n. 2587; Pallottini, *loc. cit.*

The Council of Trent and the decisions of the Sacred Congregation of the Council did not state whether the conversion of a church to profane uses would cause the church to become desecrated. Since the decree of the Council permitted only that destroyed churches be adopted for secular use, it is clear from what has been stated previously that a church whose walls were destroyed totally or in a major part became desecrated by such destruction. Hence, relative to a church which already was destroyed, at least for the greater part, such a reduction to secular status and purpose did not cause the loss of consecration for a church, because this effect was already produced by its destruction. The question, of course, could arise, namely, whether such a reduction caused the loss of consecration for a church which was destroyed only to a minor extent. It seems that the conversion to profane uses performed by the authority of the bishop did cause the church to become deprived of its consecration. Otherwise the Council of Trent would to all appearances have permitted a church to be used for profane purposes when the church still retained its original consecration or blessing. The Council of Trent evidently intended that the conversion to profane uses by the authority of the bishop would result in the loss of consecration and blessing for the church. Hence a mere declaration on the part of the bishop that a church could be used for profane purposes was sufficient for the church to lose its consecration or blessing.[28]

The Provincial Council of Auch in 1851 not only permitted the bishops to convert to profane or secular uses the churches which had fallen into ruins and could not be repaired, but also permitted the recently constructed churches to be reduced to secular status and purpose when these were found to be useless.[29]

The Council of Trent did not prescribe any specific rite for the conversion of a church to secular use, but it is evident that all sacred

[28] Cf. Many, *De Locis Sacris*, n. 27, 6°; Gasparri, *De Ssma. Eucharistia*, n. 184; Hinschius, *System des katholischen Kirchenrechts*, IV, 331; Scherer, *Handbuch des Kirchenrechts*, II, 631.

[29] C. 107—*Acta et Decreta Sacrorum Conciliorum Recentiorum, Collectio Lacensis* (7 vols., Friburgi Brisgoviae: 1870-1890), IV, 1191 (hereafter this work will be referred to as *Collectio Lacensis*).

objects were to be removed from the church before it was turned over to profane enterprises. The IV Provincial Council of Milan, held in 1576, prescribed a rite to be observed. A priest who was expressly delegated by the bishop for the ceremony was to pray in silence before the altar. He then proceeded to remove the relics from the altar, and these were reverently carried in procession to the church designated by the bishop. The clergy and the people of the church to which the relics were to be transferred took part in the procession. Later the altars were removed under the direction of the priest and likewise transferred to the neighboring church. On the following day the remains of those who were buried in the church were transferred to the neighboring church, and while this was being done the divine office for the dead was recited. A Mass of Requiem was then offered for the dead in the church to which the bodies had been transferred. Finally a cross was erected on the site of the former church and thenceforth the building could be used for secular purposes.[30] Although the observance of this rite was obligatory only in the Metropolitan See of Milan, it is probable that in other places a certain amount of ceremony was used in the removal and transfer of the sacred objects from one church to another.

Article 2. Violation of Churches

The "violation" of a church is synonymous with the "pollution" of a church. Both terms were used interchangeably throughout the history of the development of canon law. The terms were already in use before the time of the Decretals of Gregory IX, but in that earlier period the violation or pollution of a church caused the church to become desecrated, that is, to lose its consecration.[31] With the great development of the science of canon law in the twelfth and thirteenth centuries, the term "violation of a church" lost its former meaning. The Decretals of Gregory IX no longer considered the violation of a church equivalent to a loss of consecration. From this time forward the violation of a church was considered a moral

[30] Conc. IV Mediolanense, c. 20—Hardouin, X, 829.

[31] Cf. c. 139, *Excerptiones Egberti*—*MPL*, LXXXIX, 396; Mansi, XII, 426; Hardouin, III, 1974; cc. 19 and 20, D.I. *de cons.*

contamination of the sanctity of the church, which occurred as a result of certain acts committed within the church. The moral contamination continued to exist until the pristine sanctity of the church was restored by the rite of reconciliation. The acts which caused the violation of a church will be treated separately in detail below.

A. *Factors of Violation*

A) HOMICIDE

In 1207 it was related to Pope Innocent III that, as a result of a violent struggle, wounds were inflicted on some persons and homicide likewise was committed in a church. It was asked whether or not the church had to be consecrated again. The Pope replied that the church was to be reconciled by sprinkling it with water that was blessed with the admixture of wine and ashes.[32] Homicide committed in a church did not cause the church to lose its consecration, but it caused the church to become violated.[33] Thereafter this decretal was cited as the prevailing law with regard to the violation of churches by the crime of homicide.

It was the common opinion among the authors that the violation of a church resulted from homicide which was voluntary or deliberate. Hence, a church was not considered violated when a person was killed accidentally, for example, by some falling object or by a person who did not have the use of reason.[34] Furthermore, the homicide had to be unjust (*injuriosum*). Hence, if a person in self-defense killed an unjust aggressor the homicide was considered justifiable and did not cause the church to become violated, because such homicide was not considered unjust, but rather necessary.[35] Finally,the homicide had to occur in the church. Thus, if a person received a fatal blow in the church, but the subsequent death oc-

[32] C. 4, X, *de consecratione ecclesiae vel altaris,* III, 40; cf. also Augustinus, *Antiquae Decretalium Collectiones,* Comp. III, c. 3, *de dedicatione ecclesiae vel altarium,* III, 31.

[33] Panormitanus, in c. 4, X, *de consecratione ecclesiae vel altaris,* III, 40.

[34] Gonzalez-Tellez, *Commentaria . . . in Quinque Libros Decretalium,* lib. III, tit. 40, cap. 7, n. 6; Pirhing, *Ius Canonicum,* lib. III, tit. 40, n. 10; Schmalzgrueber, *Ius Ecclesiasticum Universum,* lib. III, tit. 40, n. 78.

[35] Gonzalez-Tellez, *loc. cit.;* Pirhing, *loc. cit.;* Schmalzgrueber, *ibid.,* n. 79.

curred after he had managed to leave the church, the church suffered violation none the less, for the cause of the death was locally attached to the church. But if the blow was received outside of the church, and then the person fled into the church and his death ensued therein, the church was not violated, because it was simply a death and not a homicide that had occurred in the church.[36] Again, if a person while in a church hurled a death-dealing missile at another who happened to be outside the church, it was held that a violation of the church had not taken place, for the reason that the homicide had not been perpetrated in the church. On the other hand, a church was considered to be violated if the person who threw the deadly missile was outside of the church, but killed another who was inside the church.[37] It is to be noted that homicide actually had to be verified, that is, it was necessary that death resulted, otherwise the church was not violated, regardless of the seriousness of the inflicted blow.

Just as homicide, or the killing of one person by another, violated a church, so also suicide had the same effect, provided that the person was not fully deprived of the use of his reason in the act of killing himself, otherwise self-inflicted death could not be considered voluntary and, therefore, did not violate the church.[38]

B) THE SHEDDING OF HUMAN BLOOD

That a church became violated by the shedding of human blood in the sacred building was implied in the letter of Pope Innocent III of which mention has already been made. The Pope spoke of the necessity of reconciling a church when the infliction of wounds and the perpetration of homicide had taken place in the church. Panormitanus stated that the "infliction of wounds" presupposed the shedding of blood.[39] The doctrine of Panormitanus in reality covered

[36] Barbosa, *Ius Ecclesiasticum Universum*, lib. II, cap. 4, n. 20; Gonzalez-Tellez, *loc. cit.*; Pirhing, *loc. cit.*

[37] Barbosa, *De Officio et Potestate Episcopi*, pars II, alleg. 28, n. 26; Gonzalez-Tellez, *loc. cit.*; Many, *De Locis Sacris*, n. 31, 4°.

[38] Barbosa, *Ius Ecclesiasticum Universum*, lib. II, cap. 4, n. 17; Reiffenstuel, *Ius Canonicum Universum*, lib. III, tit. 40, n. 19.

[39] In c. 4, X, *de consecratione ecclesiae vel altaris*, III, 40, n. 3.

the overwhelming majority of instances that could have come under the present heading. Conversely, however, there was common agreement among the authors that the infliction of wounds which involved bloodshed caused the violation of the church in which it was perpetrated.

The law regarding the violation of a church by bloodshed was expressly stated in a decretal of Gregory IX in 1233: "*Si ecclesia non consecrata cuiuscumque semine fuerit aut sanguinis effusione polluta, aqua protinus exorcizata lavetur, ne divinae laudis organa suspendantur; est tamen, quam citius fieri poterit consecranda.*"[40] According to this decretal a non-consecrated church became violated by bloodshed and, therefore, *a fortiori* a consecrated church became violated in the same manner.[41]

Pope Boniface VIII (1294-1303) in his decretals considered the violation of a church by bloodshed as being already definitely established in law at his time: "*Si ecclesiam pollui sanguinis aut seminis effusione contingat* . . . "[42]

Before a church became violated by the shedding of blood it was necessary that the blood be that of a human being and that the cause of the bloodshed be placed unjustly.[43] Hence Barbosa explained that if the blood of an irrational animal were shed, the church would not be considered violated, because this would not be an unjust shedding of blood, since an animal cannot be a subject of rights either actively or passively.[44]

In order to determine whether the shedding of blood effected the violation of a church it was necessary to determine in law what amount of bloodshed sufficed for bringing about such an effect. The word *effusio*, as used in the *Decretals* of Gregory IX and Boniface VIII, meant a flowing of blood. Hence, the shedding of a few drops

[40] C. 10, X, *de consecratione ecclesiae vel altaris*, III, 40.

[41] *Glossa* in c. 10, X, *de consecratione ecclesiae vel altaris*, III, 40, v. "non consecrata."

[42] C. un., *de consecratione ecclesiae vel altaris*, III, 21, in VI°.

[43] *Glossa* in c. un., *de consecratione ecclesiae vel altaris*, III, 21, in VI°, v. 'Sanguinis."

[44] *De Officio et Potestate Episcopi*, pars II, alleg. 28, n. 31; cf. Schmalzgrueber, *Ius Ecclesiasticum Universum*, lib. III, tit. 40, n. 80.

did not suffice to bring about a violation of the church; rather, a considerable flow of blood was presupposed.[45]

All authors agreed that the violation of a church ensued upon an act which caused bloodshed if the latter constituted a gravely sinful act. Pirhing adverted to the fact that the nose of a person was very sensitive and that a slight blow on the nose could very easily cause a great flow of blood. Yet, even though a large amount of blood were in this manner shed in a church as the result of a fight between small boys, the church was not violated, because an act of this kind was not considered gravely sinful.[46] Neither was a church violated if a parent, while rebuking a child for its misbehavior, struck it and caused a large amount of blood to flow from its nose.[47] The Sacred Congregation of the Council likewise declared that a church was not violated even though twenty-four drops of blood were shed as the result of a slight blow received upon the nose.[48]

Furthermore, it was requisite that the wound which caused the bloodshed be inflicted deliberately (*voluntarium*). Hence, the shedding of blood occasioned by accident or by one who did not have the use of reason, for example, by an insane person or by one who was intoxicated to such an extent that he was not aware of his action, did not cause the church to become violated.[49]

Finally, if the violation of a church was to ensue, then the cause of bloodshed had to be localized within the church in the manner already explained under the heading of homicide. It was not necessary, however, that the blood came in contact with the church itself. If the cause of the actual bloodshed was made operative on

[45] Pirhing, *Ius Canonicum*, lib. III, tit. 40, n. 11; Barbosa, *De Officio et Potestate Episcopi*, pars II, alleg. 28, n. 34; cf. *glossa* in c. un., *de consecratione ecclesiae vel altaris*, III, 21, in VI°, v. "Nota primo."

[46] *Ius Canonicum*, lib. III, tit. 40, n. 11.

[47] Barbosa, *De Officio et Potestate Episcopi*, pars II, alleg. 28, n. 36; Suarez, *Opera Omnia*, tract. *de eucharistia*, disp. LXXXI, sect. 4, n. 2; Reiffenstuel, *Ius Canonicum Universum*, lib. III, tit. 40, n. 16.

[48] S.C.C. in *Marsorum*, 18 dec. 1649—Pallottini, v. "ecclesia in' genere," § III, n. 4.

[49] Barbosa, *De Officio et Potestate Episcopi*, pars II, alleg. 28, nn. 3-5.

a person while he was within the church, then the church was violated, regardless of the fact that the blood was absorbed by the wounded person's clothing, or that the blood was allowed to flow into some vase or other receptacle.[50]

C) EFFUSIO SEMINIS

The decretals of Gregory IX and Boniface VIII expressly set forth the law that a church became violated by the *effusio seminis* occurring in a church. Pope Gregory IX stated explicitly: "*Si ecclesia non consecrata cuiuscumque semine fuerit . . . polluta, aqua protinus exorcizata lavetur . . .* "[51] Pope Boniface VIII likewise declared that a church became violated by the *effusio seminis*: "*Si ecclesiam pollui . . . seminis effusione contingat . . .* "[52] Pope Alexander III (1159-1181) declared that adultery caused the church to become violated in which it was committed.[53] With the exception of the decretal of Pope Alexander III, which explicitly stated that adultery violated a church, the other two decretals did not advert to the possible manner in consequence of which the *effusio seminis* violated a church. Since *effusio seminis* stands as a general term, it seems indicated to maintain that a church became violated regardless of the manner in which the *effusio seminis* was procured therein. All authors insisted, of course, that the *effusio* had to exist as a voluntary act before the violation of a church was thereby effected, and that correspondingly an *effusio seminis* which occurred during sleep did not involve a violation of the church.[54] It was

[50] Barbosa, *ibid.*, n. 24; Schmalzgrueber, *Ius Ecclesiasticum Universum*, lib. III, tit. 40, n. 80.

[51] C. 10, X, *de consecratione ecclesiae vel altaris*, III, 40.

[52] C. un., *de consecratione ecclesiae vel altaris*, III, 21, in VI°

[53] "Significasti nobis, quendam presbyterum cum alterius coniuge instinctu diabolico infra ecclesiam frequenter, sicut asseris, dormivisse, quae utique se et illum cuidam sacerdoti huiusmodi delictum confessos fuisse, publice tibi detexit, et hoc ipsum idem sacerdos, nomen adulteri celans, in praesentia tua dixit . . . Ideoque mandamus . . . ecclesiam praelibatam per aspersionem aquae benedictae reconciliare procures . . ."—c. 5, X, *de adulteriis et stupro*, V, 16; cf. also Augustinus, *Antiquae Decretalium Collectiones*, Comp. I, c. 6, *de adulteriis et stupro*, V, 13; Jaffé, *Regesta Romanorum Pontificum*, n. 12183.

[54] Gonzalez-Tellez, *Commentaria . . . in Quinque Libros Decretalium*, lib.

generally held by the authors that for a church to become violated the *effusio seminis* had to be illicit. Hence any sinful act such as fornication, adultery, self-pollution, sodomy, bestiality, etc. caused a church to become violated.[55]

A church was also considered to be violated if sexual intercourse between a man and his wife took place in a church, for although such an act was licit in itself, nevertheless it was considered illicit in view of the sacredness of the place in which it occurred, just as the execution of a capital sentence was considered unlawful if it was carried out in a church.[56] The exchange of marital relations within a church did not, however, cause the church to become violated under certain extreme conditions. Thus, for example, spouses who because of war or other circumstances were forced to live in a church for a long period of time did not furnish cause for the violation of a church by their exchange of marital relations, for under such conditions it could in given instances be rightfully assumed that there was danger of incontinence, and that their spiritual welfare would have been jeopardized if the lawful acts of married life had been totally denied them. Therefore, just as homicide committed in self-defense did not violate a church, so neither was a church violated by the marital relations which were exchanged for the purpose of safeguarding the spiritual welfare of the spouses.[57]

D) BURIAL OF AN INFIDEL OR OF AN EXCOMMUNICATED PERSON

Pope Innocent III in 1213 issued the following law: "*Coemeteria . . . in quibus excommunicatorum corpora sepeliri contingit . . .*

III, tit. 40 cap. 6, n. 7; Barbosa, *De Officio et Potestate Episcopi*, pars II, alleg. 28, n. 43; Pirhing, *Ius Canonicum*, lib. III, tit. 40, n. 12; Suarez, *Opera Omnia, tract. de eucharistia*, disp. LXXXI, sect. 4, n. 3.

[55] Suarez, *loc. cit.;* Barbosa, *ibid.*, n. 42; Reiffenstuel, *Ius Canonicum Universum*, lib. III, tit. 40, n. 20.

[56] Barbosa, *ibid.*, n. 47; Pirhing, *Ius Canonicum*, lib. III, tit. 40, n. 12; Sanchez, *De Matrimonio* (3 vols., Venetiis: 1614), lib. IX, disp. 15, n. 7; cf. also *glossa* in c. un., *de consecratione ecclesiae vel altaris*, III, 21, in VI°, v. "nota ulterius."

[57] Pirhing, *ibid.*, n. 12; Sanchez, *ibid.*, n. 12; Barbosa, *ibid.*, n. 48; Schmalzgrueber, *Ius Ecclesiasticum Universum*, lib. III, tit. 40, n. 81; Reiffenstuel, *ibid.*, n. 20.

reconcilianda sunt aspersione aquae solemniter benedictae, sicut in dedicationibus ecclesiarum fieri consuevit".[58] Although this decretal stated only that cemeteries were violated by the burial of excommunicated persons, authors were in agreement that churches also were violated in the same manner.[59]

The faithful were strictly forbidden to have any communication whatsoever with persons who were excommunicated. All excommunicated persons were to be avoided. This was the underlying reason for the prohibition of burying excommunicated persons with the faithful.[60] In 1418, however, at the Eucumenical Council of Constance, Pope Martin V issued his famous constitution *Ad evitanda scandala* in which it was declared that thenceforth there were to be avoided only those excommunicated persons against whom an express judicial sentence of this kind had been published, as well as those who were publicly and expressly denounced as such, and those who were notorious persecutors of the clergy.[61] After the publication of this constitution the more common opinion among authors was that a church became violated only when an *excommunicatus vitandus* was buried therein.[62]

[58] C. 7, X, *de consecratione ecclesiae vel altaris*, III, 40; cf. also Augustinus, *Antiquae Decretalium Collectiones*, Comp. IV, c. 1, *de celebratione divini officii*, III, 15.

[59] Pirhing, *Ius Canonicum*, lib. III, tit. 40, n. 13; Gonzalez-Tellez, *Commentaria . . . in Quinque Libros Decretalium*, lib. III, tit. 40, cap. 7, n. 8; Barbosa, *De Officio et Potestate Episcopi*, pars II, alleg. 28, n. 52; Reiffenstuel, *Ius Canonicum Universum*, lib. III, tit. 40, n. 21; Schmalzgrueber, *Ius Ecclesiasticum Universum*, lib. III, tit. 40, n. 67.

[60] "Quibus non communicavimus vivis non communicemus defunctis."—Innocent III in c. 12, X, *de sepulturis*, III, 28.

[61] ". . . nemo deinceps . . . teneatur abstinere, vel aliquem vitare ac interdictum observare, nisi sententia vel censura huiusmodi fuerit in vel contra personam . . . a judice publicata vel denunciata . . . [et] si quem pro sacrilegio et manuum iniectione in clerum, sententiam latam a canone adeo notorie constiterit incidisse. . . ."—Mansi, XXVII, 1192-1193; *Fontes*, n. 45.

[62] Barbosa, *ibid.*, n. 52; Pirhing, *ibid.*, n. 13; Suarez, *Opera Omnia*, tract. de *eucharistia*, disp. LXXXI, sect. 4, n. 5; Gonsalez-Tellez, *ibid.*, n. 8; Reiffenstuel, *ibid.*, n. 21; Schmalzgrueber, *ibid.*, n. 75. Gasparri (*DeSsma. Eucharistia*, n. 254) and a few others held that a church was violated also by the burial of a heretic or schismatic, even though he was not a *vitandus*.

With regard to the burial of a pagan or of an infidel there was no explicit legislation which declared that such burial would cause a church to become violated. All authors, however, were in agreement that the violation of a church resulted from the burial of an infidel therein. As a basis for their contention they cited canons 27 and 28, D. I., *de cons.*, of the *Decretum* of Gratian. These canons, as has been noted previously, were a repetition of a similar decree contained in the *Penitential* of Theodore of Canterbury. These decrees, as found in Gratian, did not obtain the force of law, but merely testified to the custom of the time, which eventually acquired the force of universal consuetudinary law.[63]

A few authors held that the burial of a catechumen violated a church, because such a person was not yet considered to be one of the faithful.[64] The more common opinion, however, was that the burial of a catechumen in a church did not violate it, because such a person was considered to be a Christian in the wide sense of the term in view of his baptism of desire.[65]

Authors did not agree regarding the violation of a church resulting from the burial of an unbaptized infant therein. Some of the canonists held that the burial in a church of unbaptized infants of infidel parents induced violation, but that the burial of infants of Christian parents did not, since such children were not to be considered infidels, but rather quasi-catechumens.[66] The more probable opinion, however, seems to have been the opinion of those authors who held that the burial of any unbaptized child violated a church, for an infant was considered to be an infidel as long as he was not baptized, regardless of the Christianity of his parents.[67] All authors

[63] Many, *De Locis Sacris*, n. 34, 2°.

[64] Zoesius, *Commentaria ad Decretales Gregorii IX*, lib. III, tit. 40, n. 13, as cited by Schmalzgrueber, *ibid.*, n. 72.

[65] Schmalzgrueber, *Ius Ecclesiasticum Universum*, lib. III, tit. 40, n. 72; Barbosa, *De Officio et Potestate Episcopi*, pars II, alleg. 28, n. 53; Many, *De Locis Sacris*, n. 34, 3°.

[66] Many, *De Locis Sacris*, n. 34, 3°; Schmalzgrueber, *Ius Ecclesiasticum Universum* lib. III, tit. 40, n. 74; Gasparri, *De Ssma. Eucharistia*, n. 253.

[67] Suarez, *Opera Omnia*, tract. de eucharistia, disp. LXXXI, sect. 4, n. 6; S. Alphonsus de Ligorio, *Theologia Moralis* (2 vols., Augustae Taurinorum:

agreed that the burial of a child still in the womb of its dead mother did not violate a church, because an unborn child was considered to be a part of the mother, and if she was a Christian the church was not considered to be violated by her burial therein.

B. *Requisite Conditions for Violation*

A. CERTAINTY REGARDING THE COMMITTED ACT

In the preceding article it has been pointed out that a church became violated when homicide, bloodshed, *effusio seminis*, or the burial of an infidel or of an *excommunicatus vitandus* occurred in the church. Before a church could be considered violated by the commission of any of those acts, however, some authors maintained that certainty with regard to the committed misdeed had to be established, that is, as long as either a doubt of law or a doubt of fact remained, the effect of the church's violation did not ensue.[68] A doubt of law exists when the existence, meaning, or extent of the obligation of the law is doubtful. There was a doubt of law, for example, with regard to the violation of a church ensuing from the burial therein of an infidel, insofar as there was no existing law that made such a provision. The only extant regulation in that regard were two spurious decrees contained in the *Decretum* of Gratian. Since the origin of those decrees was doubtful, their authenticity was likewise doubtful. Hence, the burial of an infidel in a church caused at most a doubtful violation, and therefore there was no strict obligation of reconciling the church.[69] In a doubt of fact, the law is clear, but some facts or circumstances of the case are doubtful. A doubt of fact arose, for example, when sinful acts contrary to the sixth commandment were committed in a church, but it was not certain that the *effusio seminis* actually occurred.[70]

B. NOTORIETY REGARDING THE COMMITTED ACT

A second condition that had to be verified before a church could

1891), lib. VI, n. 366; Reiffenstuel, *Ius Canonicum Universum*, lib. III, tit. 40, n. 21.

[68] Many, *De Locis Sacris*, n. 36; Gasparri, *De Ssma. Eucharistia*, n. 246.

[69] Gasparri, *loc. cit.*

[70] Gasparri, *loc. cit.*

be considered violated was that the violative act had to be notorious, that is, publicly known. This is evident from the decretal of Alexander III, where it was stated that the adultery which was committed in the church was publicly made known to the bishop (*publice tibi detexit*).[71] Thus a church was not considered to be violated if the commission of the act was not a matter of public knowledge. The violation of a church was not so much a physical contamination of the decorum which was due to the church, but rather a moral contamination of its sacred character, that is, in the judgment of men it was considered that certain specified acts were not in keeping with the dignity of the sacred place, so that when these acts were committed it was accounted that the sanctity of the church was defiled. Hence, as long as the commission of these acts was occult the church was not considered to be violated; but if their commission became publicly known at some later date the church was considered to be violated from the time at which the fact became thus known.[72]

C. LOCALIZATION OF THE COMMITTED ACT IN THE CHURCH PROPER

Finally, a third condition which had to be verified before a church could be considered violated was that the violative act took place in the church proper. The term "church" was interpreted strictly. Hence, before the violation was considered to ensue, the violative act had to occur within the part of the church in which divine services were held. This part of the church included the space between the floor and the ceiling and the entire space between the principal altar and the opposite wall. This space included also all the chapels

[71] C. 5, X, *de adulteriis et stupro*, V, 16.

[72] Cf. *glossa* in c. un., *de consecratione ecclesiae vel altaris*, III, 21, in VI°, v. "pollui"; Barbosa, *De Officio et Potestate Episcopi*, pars II, alleg. 28, n. 37; Suarez, *Opera Omnia*, tract. *de eucharistia*, disp. LXXXI, sect. 4, n. 4; Pirhing, *Ius Canonicum*, lib. III, tit. 40, n. 12; Schmalzgrueber, *Ius Ecclesiasticum Universum*, lib. III, tit. 40, n. 82; Reiffenstuel, *Ius Canonicum Universum*, lib. III, tit. 40, n. 22; Conc. Coloniense I (anno 1536), pars IX, c. 18: "Non tamen omnis pollutio hanc reconciliationem requirit, sed tantum publica vel per rei evidentiam, vel saltem per famam. Quod si occulta sit contaminatio . . . ratio reconciliationis in occultis non habet locum"—Hardouin, IX, 2017.

that were erected within the above-mentioned area.[73] Thus any rooms which perhaps existed between the ceiling and the roof were not considered part of the church. Neither was the sacristy, vestibule or portico, tower, or any adjacent room considered to be part of the church, because none of these were destined to provide space for the conduct of divine worship.[74] Hence, if any of the violative acts were committed in these places, the church was not considered violated.

A church basement containing chapels was considered part of the church, provided that access to the basement was had directly from the interior of the church proper. Such a basement consequently shared the consecration or the blessing of the church itself. Therefore, if one of the above-mentioned acts took place in this basement, the church was considered violated. However, if access to such a basement was had only from the street or from some part of the building which did not constitute the church proper, then the basement demanded its blessing or consecration as something distinct from the blessing or the consecration of the church. Thus there were constituted two distinct units; a violation of the one did not at all involve that of the other.[75]

If the basement served as a burial place and had direct communication with and access to the interior of the church, then it was considered as one with the church. Therefore any violative act which occurred in such a basement entailed for the church the same consequences that it entailed for the basement. However, if access to the basement was provided by a means other than a direct passage from the interior of the church, then the church was not affected by the consequences following upon the commission of the violative acts in the basement.[76] But if the church was violated, then the basement which served as a burial place was also violated, because a cemetery adjacent to a church shared in the violation of the church itself.[77]

[73] Pirhing, *Ius Canonicum*, lib. III, tit. 40, n. 16; Sanchez, *De Matrimonio*, lib. IX, disp. 15, n. 25.

[74] Pirhing, *loc. cit.*; Sanchez, *ibid.*, nn. 26, 28-31.

[75] Many, *De Locis Sacris*, n. 38, 3°.

[76] Many, *loc. cit.*

[77] "Si ecclesiam pollui sanguinis aut seminis effusione contingat, ipsius

Article 3. Consequences of the Violation of Churches

The decretals of Gregory IX expressly declared that a violated church was to be reconciled immediately, lest divine services should have to be discontinued.[78] Boniface VIII decreed that the violation of a church effected the violation of its adjacent cemetery and that no one was to be buried in the cemetery until the church was reconciled together with the cemetery.[79] It followed, then, that burial in a violated church was likewise prohibited until after the reconciliation of the church had taken place. It is evident from these two decretals that the violation of a church produced a threefold effect: 1. all divine services had to cease; 2. the burial of the dead was prohibited; 3. it became necessary to reconcile the church. Concerning the second effect no further explanation is required, for the meaning of the decretal is quite clear.

The enjoined cessation of divine services in the violated church implied primarily the prohibition to celebrate Mass therein. But it also entailed the prohibition of the recitation of the canonical hours in choir, the proscription of public sacred processions and the disallowance of all other liturgical functions. A cleric who contrary to this injunction nevertheless presumptuously officiated in a violated church, and thus laid himself open to serious guilt, did not, however, incur the stigma of irregularity.[80]

When the violation of a church occurred during the celebration of Mass before the Canon had begun, the Mass had to be discontinued immediately; if the violation occurred during the Canon of

coemeterium si contiguum sit eidem, censetur esse pollutum. . . Non sic quoque in casu converso sentimus, ut videlicet polluto coemeterio, quamvis ecclesiae contiguo, debet ecclesia reputari polluta, ne minus dignum maius, aut accessorium principale ad se trahere videatur."—C. un., *de consecratione ecclesiae vel altaris*, III, 21, in VI°. Cf. also Pirhing, *Ius Canonicum*, lib. III, tit. 40, n. 16; Sanchez, *De Matrimonio*, lib. IX, disp. 15, n. 27.

78 C. 10, X, *de consecratione ecclesiae vel altaris*, III, 40.

79 C. un., *de consecratione ecclesiae vel altaris*, III, 21, in VI°.

80 "Is, qui in ecclesia . . . polluta . . . scienter . . . celebrare praesumit, licet in hoc temerarie agat, irregularitatis tamen, quum id non sit expressum in iure, laqueum non incurrit"—C. 18, *de sententia excommunicationis, suspensionis et interdicti*, V, 11, in VI°. Cf. also Barbosa, *Ius Ecclesiasticum Universum*, lib. II, cap. 4, n. 33.

the Mass, the Mass was to be continued until its completion without any interruption.[81] If the violation of a church occurred during the celebration of any other divine service, then such service had to be discontinued immediately.[82]

Canonists and theologians maintained that the bishop could permit Mass to be celebrated in a violated church when there was no other church in which the faithful could fulfill their obligation of hearing Mass, and also when it was impossible to reconcile the church immediately. Furthermore, the permission of the bishop for the celebration of Mass could be presumed if it was impossible to reach him and if grave necessity demanded that Mass be celebrated.[83]

The Sacred Congregation of Indulgences declared that the indulgences which could be gained by visiting a church were not suspended or withheld during the visits that were made to a violated church. This declaration was confirmed and approved by Pope Pius IX.[84]

The reconciliation, which was a sacred rite by which a violated church was made fit again for divine services, was to be performed as soon as possible.[85] Prior to the reconciliation of a church which had become violated by the burial of an infidel, or of an *excommunicatus vitandus*, it was necessary to remove the body from the church only if it could be distinguished from the other remains of the faithful whose bodies likewise lay buried in the church; other-

[81] *Missale Romanum*, tit. *de defectibus in celebratione missarum occurrentibus*, cap. X, *de defectibus in ministerio ipso occurrentibus*, n. 2: "Si, Sacerdote celebrante, violetur Ecclesia ante Canonem, dimittatur Missa; si post Canonem, non dimittatur."

[82] Many, *De Locis Sacris*, n. 40, 3°.

[83] Suarez, *Opera Omnia*, tract. *de eucharistia*, disp. LXXXI, sect. 4, n. 8; St. Alphonsus, *Theologia Moralis*, lib. VI, n. 361; Schmalzgrueber, *Ius Ecclesiasticum Universum*, lib. III, tit. 40, n. 65; Gasparri, *De Ssma. Eucharistia*, n. 243.

[84] 18 sept. 1862, *Ordinis Carmelitarum Discalceat.—Decreta Authentica Sacrae Congregationis Indulgentiis Sacrisque Reliquiis praepositae ab anno* 1668 *ad annum* 1882 *edita iussu et auctoritate SS. D.N. Leonis PP. XIII* (Ratisbonae, Neo Eboraci, Cincinnati, 1883), n. 396 (hereafter this work will be referred to as *Decreta Authentica* S.C. *Indulg.*); *Fontes*, n. 5066.

[85] ". . . aqua protinus benedicta lavetur . . ."—C. 10, X, de *consecratione ecclesiae vel altaris*, III, 40.

wise there would have been present the imminent danger of removing one of the bodies of the faithful, which of course would have implied an unjust procedure.[86] The reconciliation was to be performed by sprinkling the walls of the church with holy water.[87] The Sacred Congregation of Rites declared that a violated church was not reconciled by the celebration of Mass therein; it was to be reconciled by the prescribed form as given in the liturgical books.[88]

Article 4. Minister of Reconciliation

A. *Consecrated Churches*

The reconciliation of a consecrated church was reserved to the local bishop. The local bishop could for the reconciliation of consecrated churches in his own territory grant permission to any other bishop. Such permission, however, could not be granted to a simple priest. These laws were given in the decretal of Gregory IX:

> "Aqua per episcopum benedicta ecclesiam reconciliari posse per alium episcopum non negamus, per sacerdotes hoc fieri de cetero prohibentes, non obstante consuetudine provinciae Bracharensis, quae dicenda est potius corruptela; quia, licet episcopus committere valeat quae iurisdictionis existunt, quae ordinis tamen episcopalis sunt non potest inferioris gradus clericis demandare. Quod autem mandantibus episcopis super reconciliatione factum est hactenus per eosdem, misericorditer toleramus."[89]

The Pope condemned the practice of some bishops who delegated simple priests to reconcile consecrated churches. In not demanding that such churches should be reconciled again it seems that the Pope validated the reconciliation which had been invalid from the beginning.[90] Gasparri,[91] in commenting upon this decretal of Gregory IX, adverted to the fact that the Pope, as the supreme legislator of

[86] Cf. c. 12, X, *de sepulturis,* III, 28.

[87] Cf. cc. 4, 7, 9, 10, X, *de consecratione ecclesiae vel altaris,* III, 40.

[88] 19 aug. 1634, *Oppiden.,* ad II— *Decr. Auth.,* n. 611; *Coll. S. C. de Prop. Fide* (ed. 1907), n. 78.

[89] C. 9, X, *de consecratione ecclesiae vel altaris,* III, 40.

[90] Cf. *glossa* in c. 9, X, *de consecratione ecclesiae vel altaris,* III, 40, v. "toleramus."

[91] *De Ssma. Eucharistia,* n. 256.

ecclesiastical law, could grant a *sanatio* for an invalid reconciliation of a church, whereby the invalid reconciliation would be considered valid.

The Sacred Congregation of Rites refused to grant faculties for simple priests to reconcile consecrated churches. It declared that the reconciliation of consecrated churches should be performed by another bishop when the local bishop was absent or impeded from performing the rite.[92] During the vacancy of a see the chapter or vicar capitular (diocesan consultors or diocesan administrator in this country) could give permission to a bishop of another diocese to reconcile a consecrated church, because these persons have the power of jurisdiction when a see becomes vacant.[93] A bishop could reconcile a church in a diocese in which he had no jurisdiction, because he had the required power of orders. The reconciliation was valid but illicit if he did not have the permission of the local bishop.[94]

The Roman Pontiff could delegate a simple priest to reconcile a consecrated church. This privilege was granted only in particular cases. In 1313 Pope Clement V granted to the Archbishop of Canterbury for a period of three years a privilege by virtue of which simple priests could be delegated by him to reconcile consecrated churches. It was required that the priests should use water which was blessed by the Archbishop of Canterbury or by some other bishop.[95]

In 1761 the cathedral chapter of the archdiocese of Salamanca wrote to the Sacred Congregation of Rites, explaining that the Cathedral church, and other churches which belonged to the University of that city, were often violated because of fights which arose among the students. It was asked that the faculty to reconcile the churches be granted to ecclesiastical dignitaries, because the see might be vacant, or the bishop might be absent and no other bishop might be available for a long time. Masses and other sacred functions

[92] *Cameracen.*, 9 feb. 1608—*Decr. Auth.*, n. 246.

[93] Gasparri, *De Ssma. Eucharistia*, n. 256.

[94] S.R.C., *Oppiden.*, 19 aug. 1634, ad II—*Decr. Auth.*, n. 611; *Coll. S.C. de Prop. Fide* (ed. 1907), n. 78.

[95] Wilkins, *Concilia Magnae Brittaniae et Hiberniae* (4 vols., Londini, 1737), II, 435.

would have to be discontinued for a long time to the great detriment of the students. Pope Clement XIII granted the following privilege through the Sacred Congregation of Rites: During the vacancy of the see, if no other bishop is in the diocese or nearby, the Vicar capitular is permitted to reconcile the churches, provided that he uses water which has been solemnly blessed by a neighboring bishop; if the bishop is impeded either through sickness or by his absence from the diocese, the first dignitary of the chapter can reconcile the churches, provided that he has the written permission from the local bishop and uses the water blessed by a bishop.[96] The water which was to be used in reconciling consecrated churches had to be solemnly blessed by a bishop. To the water which was to be solemnly blessed there had to be added a small admixture of salt, ashes and wine. The mingling of these elements with the water was to be accomplished with the properly called for liturgical prayers.[97]

Pope Leo X, by virtue of the brief "Religionis suadet" (3 febr. 1515), granted to the major superiors of the Order of Friars Minor the privilege of reconciling their own churches. The privilege also granted the faculty of solemnly blessing the water, particularly when the churches were located in remote places, from which it was necessary to travel more than forty miles in order to reach the bishop.[98] By virtue of the communication of privileges other Regular major superiors enjoyed the same privilege.[99]

B. *Blessed Churches*

A decretal of Gregory IX stated: "*Si ecclesia non consecrata* . . .

[96] S.R.C., *Salamantina*, 12 dec. 1761—*Decr. Auth.*, n. 2463.

[97] Cc. 4, 7, X, *de consecratione ecclesiae vel altaris*, III, 40.

[98] ". . . illas [ecclesias] . . . sanguinis seu seminis effusione, seu alias quomodolibet pollutas, seu polluta, quoties opus fuerit, aqua per vos, praesertim in locis remotis ubi episcopum aquam benedicentem per duas dietas adire non poteritis, benedicta, reconciliare libere et licite valeatis, auctoritate Apostolica, tenore praesentium concedimus et indulgemus . . ."—Sigismund Ferraria, *Bullarium seu Collectio Bullarum et Litterarum Apostolicarum* (6 vols., Romae: 1640-1650), VI, 217.

[99] Many, *De Locis Sacris*, n. 42, 1°, d; Vermeersch, art. IV, "De consecratione, benedictione et reconciliatione Ecclesiae religiosorum"—*Periodica*, II (1911), 192-195.

fuerit . . . polluta, aqua protinus exorcizata lavetur . . ."[100] The *glossa* interpreted this decretal as meaning that a non-consecrated church could be reconciled by a simple priest through the use of ordinary holy water. The reason for this contention was that if the Pope had intended that a non-consecrated church should be reconciled by a bishop he would have expressed it.[101]

Pope Benedict XIV and other canonists maintained that a simple priest did not have to obtain delegation from the bishop in order to reconcile an unconsecrated church.[102] The *Roman Ritual,* however, stated explicitly that a church which had not been consecrated could be reconciled by a priest who was delegated by the bishop.[103]

The reason for the difference of opinion between the authors and the Ritual lies, perhaps, in the fact that, in a declaration of the Sacred Congregation of Rites in 1608, it was stated that the simple reconciliation of a church could be committed to a priest.[104] The decree did not say that delegation was necessary, but simply stated that a priest could reconcile a church which was only blessed but not consecrated. The question was finally settled by the Sacred Congregation of Rites in 1904, when it declared that a simple priest could not by his own power reconcile a blessed church, but only by the delegation of the bishop.[105]

SUMMARY AND CONCLUSIONS

The following items seek to set down in a summary manner the conclusions that have been reached in the preceding historical study of the desecration and violation of churches.

[100] C. 10, X, *de consecratione ecclesiae vel altaris,* III, 40.

[101] *Glossa* in c. 10, X, *de consecratione ecclesiae vel altaris,* III, 40.

[102] Benedictus XIV, *De Synodo Dioecessana* (3 vols., Romae: 1788), lib. XIII, cap. 15, n. 2; Barbosa, *De Officio et Potestate Episcopi,* pars II, alleg. 28, n. 57; Pirhing, *Ius Canonicum,* lib. III, tit. 40, n. 21; Schmalzgrueber, *Ius Ecclesiasticum Universum,* lib. III, tit. 40, n. 84; Reiffenstuel, *Ius Canonicum Universum,* lib. III, tit. 40, n. 28.

[103] Tit. VIII, cap. 28, *Ritus reconciliandi ecclesiam violatam si nondum erat ab episcopo consecrata,* n. 1.

[104] *Cameracen.,* 9 feb. 1608—*Decr. Auth.,* n. 246.

[105] *Nolana,* 8 iulii 1904—*Decr. Auth.,* n. 3091; *Coll. S.C. de Prop. Fide* (ed. 1907), n. 2201; *Analecta Ecclesiastica,* XII (1904), 383.

1. Up to the time of Gratian there was no clear distinction made between the concepts of desecration and violation relative to churches. Churches lost their consecration: a) when they were completely destroyed; b) when the principal altar was destroyed or removed from the church; c) when bloodshed, homicide and *effusio seminis* occurred in the church. The burial of an infidel in a church did not cause desecration, but it seems that a church was considered violated, although this was not expressly so stated in the law.

2. A clear distinction between the desecration and violation of churches first came into use with the Decretals of Gregory IX.

3. The complete destruction of a church caused the loss of consecration.

4. The destruction of a major part of the walls desecrated a church.

5. The opinion of the authors that desecration resulted from the destruction of a major part of the plaster of the walls was declared untenable by the Sacred Congregation of Rites in 1896.

6. Desecration of a church took place when it was converted to profane uses by the authority of the bishop as authorized first by the Council of Trent.

7. Violation of churches resulted only from notorious homicide, bloodshed, *effusio seminis* and the burial of a pagan or of an *excommunicatus vitandus* in a church.

8. Divine services were forbidden in a violated church until the rite of reconciliation was performed.

9. The minister of the reconciling of a consecrated church was the bishop.

10. Simple priests could not validly reconcile consecrated churches except by express delegation from the Holy See.

11. Simple priests could licitly reconcile blessed churches only by express delegation of the bishop.

PART II
COMMENTARY

Chapter IV
DESECRATION OF CHURCHES

The desecration of a church, as has already been pointed out in the introduction to this work, may be defined as the loss of its consecration or blessing. Canon 1170 of the present Code of Canon Law provides:

> **Consecrationem vel benedictionem ecclesia non amittit, nisi tota destructa fuerit, vel maior parietum pars corruerit, vel in usus profanos ab Ordinario loci redacta sit, ad norman can. 1187.**

Prior to the Code some authors distinguished between the desecration of a consecrated church and the desecration of a blessed church. They maintained that the blessing of a church adhered to its floor *(pavimento)*, while the consecration of a church adhered to its walls. Consequently, according to their manner of theorizing, a consecrated church became desecrated when it was totally destroyed or when the greater part of the walls was destroyed; whereas, a blessed church did not become desecrated even though all of its walls were demolished in their entirety, provided the floor or the pavement was not destroyed.[1]

This opinion is no longer tenable, however, in view of the wording of the Code which rules that a church does not lose its consecration or blessing unless it is totally destroyed, or unless the greater part of its walls is destroyed or collapses. The law ex-

[1] Schmalzgrueber, *Ius Ecclesiasticum Universum*, lib. III, tit. 40, n. 16; cf. also D'Annibale, *Summula Theologia Moralis* (5 ed., 3 vols., Romae: 1908), III, n. 9 (henceforth this work will be referred to as *Theo. Mor.*); Suarez, *Opera Omnia*, tract. *de eucharistia*, disp. LXXXI, sect. IV, n. 7; Sanchez, *De Matrimonio*, lib. IX, disp. XV, n. 37; A. J. Schulte, *Benedicenda*, p. 87, footnote, n. 7.

plicitly mentions the destruction of the walls as the factor effecting the desecration of a church, but it is silent with regard to the floor, thus indicating that the destruction of the latter does not effect the desecration of a church.

It is to be borne in mind that throughout the entire treatise in the Code on the desecration of a church the term "desecration" is used with reference both to consecrated and blessed churches. This is evident from the definition of the term itself and also from the wording of canon 1170, which applies one and the same rule to both consecrated and blessed churches.

The Code lists three causes which bring about the desecration of a church: 1. the total destruction of a church; 2. the collapse or destruction of the greater part of the walls of a church; 3. the reduction of a church to secular status and purpose by the authority of the local ordinary, according to the norms given in canon 1187. The use of the word "*nisi*" indicates that the three causes enumerated constitute an exhausive list, that is, the desecration of a church cannot be effected by any cause unless it is one of the three mentioned in the law. Each of these causes will be discussed under separate headings.

Canon 1168, § 1, provides that every consecrated or blessed church must have its own title, which cannot be changed after the dedication of the church. When a church loses its consecration or blessing, however, as the result of any of the three causes mentioned in canon 1170, the title is also lost.[2] Therefore, in the rededication of a desecrated church a new title may be given to the church,[3] but the Sacred Congregation of Rites deems it more fitting that the original title be kept or, at most, that a new title be added to the old one.[4]

Article I. Total Destruction

The Code of Canon Law provides that a church becomes desecrated when it is totally destroyed,[5] and, consequently, when such

[2] Many, *De Locis Sacris*, n. 22, 2°.

[3] S.R.C., *Mantuana*, 29 mar. 1760—*Decr. Auth.*, n. 2453.

[4] S.R.C., *Isclana*, 16 ian. 1885, ad I—*Decr. Auth.*, n. 3625.

[5] Cf. can. 1170.

an edifice is rebuilt it is necessary that it be consecrated or blessed again prior to the exercise of any religious services within its confines, for such a reconstructed building is to be considered a new church.[6] This ruling of the Code is not new legislation. There is documentary evidence dating back to the fifth and sixth centuries that illustrates the then existing practice of reconsecrating churches which were rebuilt after they had previously been destroyed.[7]

With regard to the desecration of a church resulting from its total destruction, one may ask what is meant by a total destruction. What amount of destruction is necessary in order that it can be considered total in the canonical sense? The first and obvious meaning of the term "total destruction" is of course the complete demolition of the entire building so that no part of it remains standing. The Sacred Congregation of Rites issued a decision wherein it was declared that a newly reconstructed church had to be consecrated even though it was built upon the site of an old church which had previously fallen completely into ruins.[8]

There is a further possibility that a church may become destroyed to such an extent that only one wall or several small portions of the walls will remain standing, as may happen, for example, as the result of an earthquake, or as the result of demolition by bombs in time of war. The concussion brought about by the above-mentioned factors may well cause the remaining walls to be weakened structurally, so that they can not be used with any degree of safety in the reconstruction of the church. It may be accepted generally then that the term "total destruction" includes the collapse or demolition of a church, even though some portions of the walls remain standing, but must be torn down because of their weakened condition.

Augustine maintains that "it would be equal to entire destruction

[6] Can. 1165, § 1; cf. Wernz, *Ius Decretalium*, n. 441; De Angelis, *Praelectiones Iuris Canonici*, lib. III, tit. 40, n. 4; Coronata, *De Locis et Temporibus Sacris*, n. 26, 4°.

[7] Cf. De Rozière, *Liber Diurnus*, nn. XXVII and XXVIII, pp. 53 and 55; cf. also *supra*, p. 12.

[8] S.R.C., *Caesaraugustana*, 31 aug. 1872, ad I—*Decr. Auth.*, n. 3269; Gardellini, *Decr. Auth.*, n. 5508.

if the whole wall, apse and roof had been removed."[9] In support of his opinion he refers to a decision of the Sacred Congregation of Rites[10] in which it was stated that a church whose wall, apse and roof had been destroyed had to be consecrated after the necessary repairs were made.[11] It cannot be inferred on the basis of that decision, however, that the destruction of one wall, the apse and the roof can be considered the equivalent of a total destruction, for it is evident from the facts presented in the case that the remaining walls were not torn down and subsequently reconstructed, but that only the deficient parts were rebuilt. The fact that the Sacred Congregation insisted upon the reconsecration of the church proves beyond doubt that the consecration of the church was lost. This result was effected not by the total destruction of the church, but rather by the destruction of the major part of the walls, which is another cause that produces desecration, as will be explained in the following article.

When a church is totally destroyed by a fortuitous occurrence of circumstances, such as fire, earthquake, bombardment, etc., or when a church is deliberately razed with the intention of rebuilding it, the consecration or blessing is lost by such a destruction. If the destroyed church were later rebuilt from the same material that had been used in its original construction, it would be necessary to consecrate or bless the church again, because the restored building does not retain the consecration or blessing of the former building. Desecration results when the church ceases to be a building, and although the same materials were used to reconstruct the church in its original form, it can no longer be said to be the same building, but rather it is an entirely new building.[12] Hence such a reconstructed building must be consecrated or blessed in the same manner as a new church.

[9] *A Commentary on the New Code of Canon Law,* VI, 32.

[10] Augustine, *ibid.*, footnote, n. 61.

[11] S.R.C., *Aretina,* 4 sept. 1875, ad II—*Decr. Auth.*, n. 3372; Gardellini, *Decr. Auth.*, n. 5632.

[12] Reiffenstuel, *Ius Canonicum Universum*, lib. III, tit. 40, n. 11; Schmalzgrueber, *Ius Ecclesiasticum Universum*, lib. III, tit. 40, n. 25; Barbosa, *De Officio et Potestate Episcopi*, pars II, alleg. 27, n. 15; Ferraris, *Prompta Bibliotheca*, v. "ecclesia," art. 4, n. 19.

Article II. Destruction of the Major Part of the Walls

The second cause which brings about the desecration of a church, according to canon 1170, is the destruction of the major part of its walls. In determining the desecration of a church as resulting from the destruction of the walls one must give consideration to the quantity destroyed rather than to the relative position of the destroyed parts of the walls. The front of the church, *i.e.*, the apse, sanctuary, and altars, is deemed to be the principal part of the building. The desecration of a church, however, is not determined by the importance of the part of the church which is destroyed, but rather by the amount of the area of the destroyed walls.[13] Since the law specifically mentions the destruction of the greater part of the walls as being required to cause the desecration of a church, the calculations must be made mathematically. The principle, therefore, which must be applied in determining the desecration of a church is that the destruction or collapse of the slightest amount greater than one half of the total area of the walls of the church would cause the church to lose its consecration or blessing. Thus the destruction of any small portion of the walls does not cause a church to become desecrated. The Sacred Congregation of Rites has declared on several occasions that a church did not have to be reconsecrated when the destroyed part of the wall was comparatively smaller than the part which still remained standing.[14]

It is to be noted further that in order to consider a church desecrated because of the destruction of its walls, the collapse of the major part of the walls must occur at one time; or if several small

[13] Barin, "Commentarium ad Canones Iuris Canonici sacram Liturgiam Spectantes"—*Ephemerides Liturgicae*, XXXVIII (1924), 231 (henceforth this article will be referred to as "Commentarium"); Coronata, *Institutiones Iuris Canonici* (5 vols., Taurini (Italia): ex Officina Libraria Marietti, Vol. II, 2. ed., *De Rebus*, 1939), n. 741, b.

[14] S.R.C., *Marianopolitana*, 20 feb. 1874—*Decr. Auth.*, n. 3326; Gardellini, *Decr. Auth.*, n. 5578; *Coll. S.C. de Prop. Fide* (ed. 1907), n. 1411; S.R.C., *Marianopolitana*, 11 mar. 1871—*Decr. Auth.*, n. 3240; *Coll. S.C. de Prop. Fide* (ed. 1907), n. 1367; S.R.C., *Barcinonen.*, 16 ian. 1886, ad I—*Decr. Auth.*, n. 3651; Gardellini, *Decr. Auth.*, n. 5959.

portions of the walls, which when added together would amount to a greater part of the walls, were to collapse at various intervals of time, it would be requisite that the successive destruction occur before the preceding destroyed part was rebuilt; otherwise, only a smaller section of the walls would be in the state of ruins at one given period of time and this would not be sufficient to cause the church to become desecrated.[15]

It is the common opinion among authors that a church does not lose its consecration or blessing when small portions of its walls are destroyed at various times and are immediately rebuilt, even though this is done with the intention of rebuilding the entire church, provided that at no one time the destroyed portion consists of the major part of the building.[16] As long as the greater part of the building remains standing, a church retains its consecration or blessing; the small reconstructed portion of the building need not be consecrated or blessed, because it automatically acquires that status by its addition to that part of the building which retains its consecration or blessing, according to the principle: *Accessorium naturam sequi congruit principalis.*[17]

When a church is enlarged as the result of one operation, in length, breadth or height, it loses its consecration or blessing if the new part is larger than the original building.[18] If, however, a church is enlarged by numerous small additions made successively and at

[15] Barin, "Commentarium"—*Ephemerides Liturgicae*, XXXVIII (1924), 231; Coronata, *Institutiones Iuris Canonici*, n. 741, b.

[16] De Meester, *Juris Canonici et Juris Canonico-Civilis Compendium* (nova ed., 3 vols. in 4, Brugis: Desclée de Brouwer et Si., 1921-1928), n. 1131, 1°, a (hereafter this work shall be referred to as *Compendium*); Coronata, *De Locis et Temporibus Sacris*, n. 26, 2°, b; Gasparri, De Ssma. Eucharistia, n. 181; Many, *De Locis Sacris*, n. 27, 4°; Reiffenstuel, *Ius Canonicum Universum*, lib. III, tit. 40, n. 12; Schmalzgrueber, *Ius Ecclesiasticum Universum*, lib. III, tit. 40, n. 28.

[17] Reg. 42, R. J., in VI°; cf. also Coronata, *De Locis et Temporibus Sacris*, n. 26, 2°, b.

[18] De Meester, *Compendium*, n. 1131, 1°, b; Pirhing, *Ius Canonicum*, lib. III, tit. 40, n. 9; Reiffenstuel, *Ius Canonicum Universum*, lib. III, tit. 40, n. 14; Schmalzgrueber, *Ius Ecclesiasticum Universum*, lib. III, tit. 40, n. 29; *Consultation III*, n. 2—*Nouvelle Revue Théologique*, XIII (1881), 322.

diverse times, it does not lose its consecration or blessing even though eventually the church is entirely rebuilt and enlarged so considerably that all vestiges of the walls of the original building are completely destroyed and removed.[19]

Prior to the Code it was the more common opinion among the canonists that a church became desecrated when the plaster that covered the surface of the interior of the walls was removed or destroyed either totally or to a major degree, even if the walls themselves did not collapse. The pre-Code canonists contended that, since the surface of the walls was anointed with chrism at the time of the consecration of a church, the consecration was lost with the destruction or removal of the plaster.[20] In view of the recent decisions of the Sacred Congregation of Rites on the matter this opinion can no longer be held.[21] It must now be maintained that if the interior is renovated and all of the plaster is removed and the walls are recovered with plaster or other material, the church does not need a new consecration or blessing, for the entire wall, not merely the surface, is consecrated or blessed.

The Sacred Congregation of Rites has always insisted in its decrees that the crosses, when removed from the walls, must be replaced as evidence of the consecration of a church.[22] The strictly

[19] S. R. C., *Caesaraugustana*, 31 aug. 1872, ad II—*Decr. Auth.*, n. 3269; cf. also S. R. C., *Barcinonen.*, 16 ian. 1886, ad II—*Decr. Auth.*, n. 3651; De Meester, *loc. cit.*; Ayrinhac, *Administrative Legislation*, p. 19; Augustine, A *Commentary*, VI, 33.

[20] Benedictus XIV, ep. "*Iam inde*", 12 maii 1754, § 7—*Fontes*, n. 440; Pirhing, *Ius Canonicum*, lib. III, tit. 40, n. 8; Reiffenstuel, *Ius Canonicum Universum*, lib. III, tit. 40, n. 13; Schmalzgrueber, *Ius Ecclesiasticum Univsum*, lib. III, tit. 40, n. 23; Hinschius, *System des katholischen Kirchenrechts*, IV, p. 331; Scherer, *Handbuch des Kirchenrechts*, II, 631.

[21] Cf. S. R. C., *Senien. et Modrussen.*, 4 maii 1882—*Decr. Auth.*, n. 3545; *Le Canoniste Contemporain*, XVIII (1895), 239; S. R. C., *Tridentina*, 11 ian. 1894—ASS, XXVII (1894-95), 439; *AER*, XII (1895), 344; *Analecta Ecclesiastica*, III (1895), 27; S. R. C., *Decretum*, 19 maii 1896, dubium II—*Decr. Auth.*, n. 3907; Coll. S. C. *de Prop. Fide* (ed. 1907), n. 1932; *Analecta Ecclesiastica*, IV (1896), 345; *Collationes Brugenses*, I (1896), 563-564; S. R. C., *Nicoteren. et Tropien.*, 9 aug. 1897, ad I—*Decr. Auth.*, n. 3962; *Le Canoniste Contemporain*, XX (1897), 710.

[22] S. R. C., *Ianuen.*, 18 feb. 1696—*Decr. Auth.*, n. 1939; *Senien. et Mod-*

liturgical prescriptions of those decrees, though not expressly referred to in the Code, remain in force in virtue of the general norm given in canon 2.[23]

Article III. Reduction to Secular Status and Purpose

That the Holy See is opposed to the reduction of churches to secular uses is evident from the prescriptions of canon 1165, § 2, whereby the local ordinary is forbidden to give his consent to the erection of a church, or, if it already is built, to its consecration or blessing, when it can prudently be foreseen that in the course of time it will be used for secular purposes. Occasionally it may happen that unforeseen circumstances will necessitate the reduction of a church to a secular status and purpose. According to canon 1170 a church loses its consecration or blessing when the local ordinary reduces a church to secular uses in accordance with the norms given in canon 1187, which rules:

> **Si qua ecclesia nullo modo ad cultum divinum adhiberi possit et omnes aditus interclusi sint ad eam reficiendam, in usum profanum non sordidum ab Ordinario loci redigi potest, et onera cum reditibus titulusque paroeciae, si ecclesia sit paroecialis, in aliam ecclesiam ab eodem Ordinario transferantur.**

In any attempt to explain the ruling of this law it is advisable to repeat in full the decree of the Council of Trent, upon which the present law is based, and to compare the present with the older legislation.

> Quum illud quoque valde curandum sit, ne ea, quae sacris ministeriis dicata sunt, temporum iniuria absolescant et

russen., 4 maii 1882—*Decr. Auth.*, n. 3545; *Nitrien.*, 13 iulii 1833, ad II—*Decr. Auth.*, n. 3584; *Barcinonen.*, 16 ian. 1886—*Decr. Auth.*, n. 3651.

[23] Codex, plerumque, nihil decernit de ritibus et caeremoniis quas liturgici libri, ab Ecclesia Latina probati, servandas praecipiunt in celebratione sacrosancti Missae sacrificii, in administratione Sacramentorum et Sacramentalium aliisque sacris peragendis. Quare *omnes liturgicae leges vim suam retinent,* nisi earum aliqua in Codice expresse corrigatur (Italics inserted by the present writer).

> ex hominum memoria excidant, episcopi, etiam tamquam apostolicae sedis delegati, transferre possint beneficia simplicia, etiam iuris patronatus, ex ecclesiis, quae vetustate vel alias collapsae sint, et ob eorum inopiam nequeant instaurari, vocatis iis, quorum interest, in matrices aut alias ecclesias locorum eorundem seu viciniorum arbitrio suo; atque in eisdem ecclesiis erigant altaria vel capellas sub eisdem invocationibus, vel in iam erecta altaria vel capellas transferant cum omnibus emolumentis et oneribus prioribus ecclesiis impositis. Parochiales vero ecclesias, etiam si iuris patronatus sint, ita collapsas refici et instaurari procurent ex fructibus et proventibus quibuscunque, ad easdem ecclesias quomodocunque pertinentibus. Qui si non fuerint sufficientes, omnes patronos et alios, qui fructus aliquos ex dictis ecclesiis provenientes percipiunt, aut, in illorum defectum, parochianos omnibus remediis opportunis ad praedicta cogant, quacunque appellatione, exemptione et contradictione remota. Quod si nimia egestate omnes laborent, ad matrices seu viciniores ecclesias transferantur, cum facultate tam dictas parochiales quam alias ecclesias dirutas in profanos usus non sordidos, erecta tamen ibi cruce, convertendi.[24]

Canon 1170 states explicitly that a church loses its consecration or blessing when it is converted to secular use by the authority of the local ordinary. The Council of Trent, although it permitted a church to be converted to secular purposes, did not state whether such conversion caused the desecration of the church. The pre-Code authors, however, maintained that the desecration of a church was effected as the result of its conversion by the bishop to secular uses.[25] That opinion seems to be implied in the Tridentine decree, for it would be repugnant to the sacred character of the church to permit it to be used for non-religious purposes when it was still dedicated to God exclusively for religious worship. The use of a church for secular purposes, furthermore, would be a violation of the legal principle of Boniface VIII: *Semel Deo dicatum, non est*

[24] Sess. XXI, *de ref.*, c. 7.

[25] Hinschius, *System des katholischen Kirchenrechts*, IV, 331; Scherer, *Handbuch des Kirchenrechts*, II, 631; Many, *De Locis Sacris*, n. 27, 6°; Gasparri, *De Ssma. Eucharistia*, I, n. 184.

ad usus humanos ulterius transferendum,[26] unless the sacred character, which was given to a church at the time of its dedication, was removed prior to its conversion to secular purposes.

With regard to the person who may permit a church to be converted to secular uses, the Council of Trent granted this power to bishops. Canon 1187 grants the same power to the local ordinary. The local ordinary is to be here understood according to the meaning indicated in canon 198, that is, within their respective territories the residential bishop, abbot and prelate *nullius,* and their vicars general, the Apostolic administrator, Apostolic vicar and prefect, as well as those who during the vacancy of the above offices succeed in the government of the respective territories according to the provisions of law. Hence, exempt major religious superiors cannot grant permission to convert a church to secular uses, even though the church is subject to the religious community, because such religious superiors are not classified under the heading of local ordinaries according to canon 198, § 2.[27] Nor does it seem probable that the vicar general can without a special mandate grant permission to reduce a church to secular purposes,[28] even though he is a local ordinary. Canon 1162, § 1, states that the written consent of the local ordinary must be obtained before a new church may be erected, but the vicar general cannot give such a consent without a special mandate. Therefore, since the local ordinary, with the exception of the vicar general, is the sole judge in determining the necessity or advisability of building a new church, by analogy with canon 1162, § 1, he should also be the sole judge with regard to determining the existence of the causes which justify the reduction of a church to secular uses.[29]

[26] Reg. 51, R. J., in VI°.

[27] Cappello, without stating on what grounds he makes his assertion, claims that if a church is only blessed the exempt major religious superior, if he blessed it personally or through a delegate, can reduce it to secular uses.—*Tractatus Canonico-Moralis De Sacramentis* (3 vols. in 6, Taurinorum Augustae, Officina Libraria Marietti: Romae), I (3. ed., 1938), n. 746 (henceforth this work will be referred to as *De Sacramentis*).

[28] Coronata holds the opposite opinion—cf. *Institutiones Iuris Canonici,* n. 741.

[29] "Omnis res, per quascumque causas nascitur, per easden dissolvitur"—c. 1, X, *de regulis iuris,* V, 41.

When an unauthorized agent subjects a church to secular usage it does not lose its consecration or blessing, and consequently does not have to be dedicated again to divine worship; at most, such an unlawful usage would cause a church to become violated.[30]

Some of the recent authors are of the opinion that the Council of Trent prescribed that a church was to be demolished when it was in a state of ruins and when sufficient funds for the restoration of the edifice were not available.[31] There is no basis for the contention that the demolition of the destroyed church was necessary, although it is evident from the Tridentine decree that the complete destruction of the church was permissible.

The Council of Trent prescribed that simple benefices, as well as all obligations along with whatever emoluments they possessed, which were attached to the destroyed church were to be transferred to the mother church, or to a neighboring church. An altar or chapel was to be erected in the mother church or a neighboring church under the same title as the destroyed church, and a cross was to be erected upon the site of the former church. The present law for the most part reiterates the Tridentine prescriptions, but it also makes some changes which indicate that the Code is less exacting than the former law. The Code simply states that "the obligations ,the revenues, and the title of the parish, if it is a parochial church, shall be transferred to another church." [32] The Code no longer insists that the obligations, such as foundation Masses, celebration of the titular feast, etc., be transferred to the mother church or to a neighboring church; the obligations may now be transferred to any church within the territory which is subject to the jurisdic-

[30] Coronata, *Institutiones Iuris Canonici*, n. 741; Ayrinhac, *Administrative Legislation*, p. 20; Augustine, *A Commentary on the New Code of Canon Law*, VI, 33; Beste, *Introductio in Codicem*, p. 563. The violation of a church resulting from its subjection to impious and sordid uses is treated in chap. V, art. I, C—cf. *infra*. pp. 76-80.

[31] De Meester, *Compendium*, n. 1144, 2°; Feldhaus, *Oratories*, Catholic University of America Canon Law Studies, n. 42, Washington, D. C.: (Catholic University of America, 1927), p. 88; Coronata, *De Locis et Temporibus Sacris*, n. 62, 2°; Ayrinhac, *Administrative Legislation*, p. 39.

[32] Cf. canon 1187.

tion of the local ordinary. It is not any longer necessary to erect an altar or chapel in the church to which the obligations have been transferred. The title of the former destroyed church must be transferred to another church, not in all instances as prescribed by the Council of Trent, but only when the former church was a parochial church. The church thus acquiring a new title retains its original title and assumes the newly added title as of equal importance with the first.[33] The obligation imposed by canon 1168, § 2, that of celebrating the titular feast annually, must then be observed on the days of the two distinctive feasts.

Although the present legislation does not provide, as the former law did, that a cross should be erected upon the site of the former church, it is fitting that this be done "lest those things which have been dedicated to sacred services may, through the injury of time, . . . pass from the memory of men . . . "[34]

The mere declaration on the part of the local ordinary that a church may be reduced to a secular status and thereupon may be used for secular purposes is sufficient in itself to cause the church to lose its consecration or blessing. The decree of the local ordinary, although it is not prescribed by the Code, should be given in writing and a copy of the document should be kept in the diocesan archives as evidence that the conversion to secular uses was performed by the proper ecclesiastical authority.

The Code does not prescribe any rite to be employed in reducing a church to a secular status. However, since a great deal of solemnity is manifested at the dedication of a church, it seems fitting that at least some liturgical function should also take place at the reduction of a church to a secular status. Moretti[35] suggests a rite which is substantially the same as that prescribed by the IV Provincial Council

[33] Cf. Gasparri, *De Ssm̃a. Eucharistia,* I, n. 139.

[34] Sess. XXI, *de ref.,* c. 7—Waterworth, *The Canons and Decrees of the Sacred and Oecumenical Council of Trent* (London: 1848), p. 149.

[35] *Caeremoniale iuxta Ritum Romanum seu De Sacris Functionibus* (4 vols., Taurini: Marietti, 1936-1939), n. 3074 (henceforth this work will be referred to as *De Sacris Functionibus*); cf. also "Breviora Responsa"—*Ephemerides Liturgicae,* XXVII (1913), 676-677.

of Milan in 1576.[36] The suggested ceremony is to be carried out in the following manner.

I. Several days before the reduction of the church to a secular status, the bodies or relics of the saints, if the church possesses any, are to be transferred to another previously selected place. The priest who performs the ceremony is to be vested in a surplice and a red stole; kneeling before the bodies or relics he recites an antiphon and an oration in honor of each saint whose remains are present. These are then carried in procession to the selected place; during the procession hymns and canticles are to be recited as prescribed by the *Roman Ritual*.[37]

II. The priest then proceeds to remove the relics of the saints from the altar in the following manner:

a) Vested in surplice and purple stole, the priest kneels before each altar, praying silently; he then recites an oration to the saint in whose honor the altar was dedicated ;

b) All the linens and ornaments are removed from the altar. The table *(mensa)* is then removed, washed and wiped dry;

c) The cavity containing the relics is opened, and the relics are removed and deposited in a decent and safe place.

If the altar is not consecrated, the consecrated altar stone is removed intact and placed in the sacristy.

III. If the church is consecrated the twelve crosses are removed from the walls.

IV. If any bodies of the faithful are buried in the church these are to be removed while the *De Profundis* is being recited, and then buried elsewhere (the IV Provincial Council of Milan prescribed that a Mass of Requiem be said in the church to which the bodies were transferred).

V. The sacred images and all ornaments are to be removed; a cross is to be erected in some convenient place in the church in a secure manner so that it cannot be easily removed. The church may then be converted to profane uses.

[36] C. 20—Hardouin, X, 829.

[37] Cf. *Rituale Romanum*, tit. IX, cap. 14, *De Processione in Translatione Sacr. Reliquiarum*.

The Code and the Council of Trent employ the words "*in usum profanum non sordidum.*" The purpose to which a church may be put, therefore, should be honest and decent; it could be used as a school, a hall for business and social assemblies, a library, an orphanage, or for any other becoming purpose. It is not permissible to employ a desecrated church as a barn or as a place for the stabling of animals. Such uses would be considered sordid.[38] When a church has been reduced to a secular status it may also become the object of sale,[39] but before the contract is completed proper precautions should be taken lest the new owner subject the building to sordid uses. The rules governing the alienation of ecclesiastical goods must also be observed.[40]

Relative to the conditions under which the local ordinary could reduce a church to a secular status and use it for secular purposes, the Council of Trent required that the church be in a state of ruin and that it could not be repaired because of the poverty of the church itself and the poverty of those upon whom normally rested the obligation of repairing it. The Code, on the other hand, states the conditions in general terms, namely, that the church can in no manner be used any longer for divine services and, secondly, that all possible means for its repair are wanting. The impossibility of repairing a church may be due to an absolute lack of funds for making the necessary but yet possible repairs, or it may be due to the fact that even though the funds are available, the building is so dilapidated that an entirely new building is necessary, mere repair no longer being possible.[41]

The question arises whether the local ordinary can licitly reduce a church to a secular status and purpose even though the two conditions mentioned in canon 1187 are not verified. It may happen at times that other causes may present themselves in justification of

[38] Cf. Blat, *Commentarium Textus Codicis Iuris Canonici* (5 vols. in 6, Romae: ex Typographia Pontificia in Instituto Pii IX, 1921-1927), III, n. 38 (henceforth this work will be referred to as *Commentarium*); De Meester, *Compendium*, n. 1144, 5°.

[39] De Meester, *ibid.*, 2°; Beste, *Introductio in Codicem*, p. 571.

[40] Cf. canons 1530-1532.

[41] Feldhaus, *Oratories*, p. 88.

such a procedure. Examples of this kind can be found in the decisions of the Sacred Congregation of the Council. In one instance a public oratory was situated upon an estate and owned by a private individual. The owner made his residence elsewhere and permission was granted for the celebration of Mass in an oratory at the new place of residence. The old public oratory, although well preserved, was not used for religious services for a period of twelve years, and the owner subjected it to secular purposes without an ecclesiastical approval. The estate itself was sold, and, desiring to sell the public oratory also, the owner petitioned the bishop for permission to reduce the oratory to a secular status in order to be able to sell the property. Upon submission of the facts to the Holy See the Sacred Congregation of the Council decided that the bishop could permit the oratory to be reduced to a secular status and subsequently sold.[42]

In another case it was demonstrated that a small rural church, situated more than two miles from town, was used only a few times a year for religious services. Because of its isolated location, the building was frequently used as a hiding place for bandits and other evil-doers who wrought considerable damage to the interior of the church and its contents. No funds were available to maintain the church properly. In view of these circumstances the Sacred Congregation of the Council issued a declaration whereby the bishop could reduce the church to a secular status and purpose.[43]

The Provincial Council of Auch in 1851 decreed that, with the approval of the bishop, churches that had fallen into ruin and could not be repaired, as well as newly constructed churches that were found to be of no use any longer, could be converted to secular but not sordid uses.[44] In giving its approval to the decrees of that

[42] S. C. C., *Ariminen*, 20 maii 1854 et 26 aug. 1854—*Thesaurus Resolutionum Sacrae Congregationis Concilii* (167 vols., Romae: 1718-1908), CXIII (1854), 225-231, 372-376; Pallottini, v. "ecclesia in genere," § II, n. 26. For another example with strikingly similar circumstances cf. S. C. C., *Bituntina*, 22 dec. 1866—*Fontes*, n. 4205.

[43] S. C. C., *Terracinen.*, 14 aprilis 1764 et 2 iunii 1764—*Thesaurus Resolutionum Sacrae Cong. Concilii*, XXXIII (1764) 68-70, 85; Pallottini, *ibid.*, n. 28.

[44] Conc. Prov. Auscitanum, c. 107—*Collectio Lacensis*, IV, 1191.

council [45] the Holy See was apparently not opposed to having bishops authorize the reduction of churches to a secular status, even though the conditions set forth by the Council of Trent were not present. This was no indication, however, that bishops could follow such a course of procedure arbitrarily; a just cause had to be present before a bishop could licitly convert a church to secular use.[46]

It seems probable that the principles which were in force prior to the Code are still applicable to the present law. Hence, even though the two conditions mentioned in canon 1187 are not verified, the local ordinary can licitly proceed with the conversion of a church to a secular status and purpose when a just cause is present. Thus, for example, a justifying cause would be the case of a church's being abandoned completely, which oftentimes may happen as the result of the people leaving the community in search of better economic conditions. Another similar example is that of a parochial church the parishioners of which have decreased in number to such an extent that the total revenues of the parish are not sufficient to meet the expenditures of the parish and no future amelioration of conditions is foreseen. Under such circumstances the local ordinary can unite the parish to another parish in such a manner that the two form only one parish, the former parish ceasing to exist as a distinct juridical entity (*unio exstinctiva*).[47] The church of the extinct parish will then be considered abandoned and it can licitly be reduced to secular purposes. Still another example of a justifying cause for converting a church to secular uses is that of a church which is too small to admit the multitude of people who should regularly attend religious services there,[48] when another church is built which is sufficiently large in itself to accommodate the large number of people. The small church, if it is no longer used for religious services, can then be converted to secular uses.

[45] Cf. *Collectio Lacensis*, IV, 1166-1167.

[46] Cf. Conc. Prov. Viennense, anno 1858, tit. IV, c. 2: "Nulla ecclesia, nullum sacellum publicum absque justa causa et Episcopi auctoritate diruatur vel ad usus profanos convertatur"—*Collectio Lacensis*, V, 179.

[47] Cf. canon 1419, 1°.

[48] Beste contends that a situation of this kind is equivalent to the condition prescribed by the Code ("si nullo modo ad cultum divinum adhiberi possit")—*Introductio in Codicem*, p. 571.

Chapter V

VIOLATION OF CHURCHES

There is a radical difference between the desecration and the violation of a church. By desecration a church loses its consecration or blessing, whereas by violation a church retains its consecration or blessing, but the effects of the consecration or of the blessing are temporarily suspended. Such suspension is caused by certain acts, specified in law, that have been committed in the church. The suspension of the effects of consecration or of blessing entails the prohibition to celebrate divine services in the church until the sacred rite of reconciliation has been performed.[1]

The violation of a church may be defined as an injury inflicted by certain acts, specified in law and committed in the church, which blemish the sacred character of the church and render it unfit for divine services until the blemish is removed by the sacred rite of reconciliation.[2] The injury that is inflicted upon a church by violation is not physical, but rather moral. De Meester calls the violation of a church a moral contamination of its sanctity, that is, the committed acts are so repugnant to the sanctity of the church that it is not fitting that divine services be celebrated therein until the contamination has been expurgated by reconciliation.[3]

Prior to the Code it was the more common opinion that not only consecrated and blessed churches, but also those churches that were not yet dedicated to divine worship by a distinct rite were subject to violation.[4] The authors who held that opinion based their contention upon the decretal of Gregory IX which ruled that if a nonconsecrated church was violated it was to be reconciled as soon as possible so that divine services would not be discontinued for a long

[1] Cf. canon 1173, § 1.

[2] Cf. De Angelis, *Praelectiones Iuris Canonici*, lib. III, tit. 40, n. 4.

[3] *Compendium*, n. 1130; cf. Bouuaert-Simenon, *Manuale Juris Canonici* (3 vols., Gandae et Leodii: H. Dessain, 1930-1931, Vol. III, 3 ed., 1931), III, n. 17.

[4] Many, *De Locis Sacris*, n. 39, 2°; D'Annibale, *Theologia Moralis*, III, n. 15; cf. Gasparri, *De Ssma. Eucharistia*, n. 247.

time.[5] It was maintained that the churches designated in that decretal could not have been blessed, because the blessing of churches was unknown at the time of Gregory IX. The pre-Code authors contended that due to the fact that bishops permitted divine services to be celebrated in churches before their consecration, such non-consecrated churches were dedicated (not by a liturgical rite, however) to divine worship, and thereby were considered to be sacred places, and as such they were subject to violation.[6]

In accordance with the law now in force sacred places are defined as those places which are set apart for divine worship, or for the burial of the dead, by a consecration or a blessing prescribed for this purpose by the approved liturgical books.[7] The canonists of today are unanimous in admitting the possibility of violation as obtaining only relative to the places that are designated as sacred in law, so that churches which are neither consecrated nor blessed cannot be subject to violation.[8] Canon 1165, § 1, rules that the celebration of divine services is forbidden in a church before the church has been consecrated or blessed. Canon 1173, § 1, provides that the celebration of divine services is forbidden in a violated church before the rite of reconciliation has been performed. Thus the canonical effect of violation is already present in a non-consecrated or unblessed church, namely, the prohibition to hold divine services therein. It follows, therefore, that there can be no violation of a non-consecrated or unblessed church, for before its dedication to divine worship by consecration or blessing a church edifice, from a canonical viewpoint, is no different from any other building.

It is noteworthy at this point to make a few observations regarding oratories. The Code does not provide any specific legislation concerning the violation of oratories, but canon 1191, § 1, applies to public oratories all the laws that govern churches.[9] The consecration

[5] C. 10, X, *de consecratione ecclesiae vel altaris,* III, 40.

[6] Cf. Many, *loc. cit.*

[7] Canon 1154.

[8] Vermeersch-Creusen, *Epitome Iuris Canonici* (3 vols., Mechlinae-Romae: H. Dessain, 1934-1937), II (5. ed., 1934), n. 489; Coronata, *De Locis et Temporibus Sacris,* n. 28, 4°; Augustine, *A Commentary,* VI, 40.

[9] "Oratoria publica eodem iure quo ecclesiae reguntur."

of a public oratory is not prescribed by law, but it is permitted.[10] If it is not consecrated, a public oratory must be blessed, otherwise divine services cannot be celebrated therein.[11] By their consecration or blessing, therefore, public oratories are constituted sacred places, and as such they are subject to violation in the same manner as consecrated or blessed churches.[12]

The possibility of semi-public oratories being subject to violation depends upon whether or not they are consecrated or blessed after the manner of churches. It is not required by law that such oratories be consecrated or blessed in a solemn manner; they may be blessed with the so-called *benedictio loci* or the *benedictio domus novae.*[13] Such a blessing, however, is merely invocative and does not constitute a semi-public oratory as a sacred place; hence, such an oratory is not subject to violation.[14]

Private oratories, that is, domestic oratories and cemetery chapels, likewise are not subject to violation, because they are not sacred places.[15] Such oratories are not blessed or consecrated like churches, but they may receive the *benedictio loci* or the *benedictio domus novae.*[16]

It must be noted that the commission of a violative act brings about the violation of a consecrated or blessed church, even though there is ignorance of the ensuing violation on the part of the person who has committed the evil deed, for the violation of a church does not have the nature of a canonical penalty, which demands that knowledge of the penalty must be had before it can be incurred. Neither is it required for the violation of the church to be effected that the violative act be placed as formally injurious to the sacred place; the mere commission of the designated and specified act causes

[10] Cf. canons 1165, § 3, and 1191, § 1.

[11] Canons 1191, § 1, and 1165, § 1.

[12] Coronata, *De Locis et Temporibus Sacris,* n. 28, 4°, b.

[13] Canon 1196, § 2; *Rituale Romanum,* tit. VIII, c. 6, *Benedictio loci* and c. 7, *Alia benedictio domus novae.*

[14] Cf. Vermeersch-Creusen, *Epitome,* II, n. 489.

[15] Cf. Augustine, *A Commentary,* VI, 83; Coronata, *De Locis et Temporibus Sacris,* n. 28, 4°, c.

[16] Canon 1196, §§ 1, 2.

the church to become violated, even though the agent had no intention of bringing about such an effect.[17]

The pre-Code discipline relative to the violation of churches ruled that when a church was violated the adjacent cemetery was also to be considered as violated.[18] The Code now rules that a cemetery becomes violated by the commission therein of the acts which violate a church,[19] but the violation of a church no longer entails the violation of an adjoining cemetery, nor does the violation of a cemetery involve the violation of the church which it adjoins.[20]

The specified acts and the conditions under which the violation of a church is effected are enumerated in canon 1172, § 2:

> **Ecclesia violatur infra recensitis tantum actibus, dummodo certi sint, notorii, et in ipsa ecclesia positi:**
> **1°. Delicto homicidii;**
> **2°. Iniuriosa et gravi sanguinis effusione;**
> **3°. Impiis vel sordidis usibus, quibus ecclesia addicta fuerit;**
> ....
> **4°. Sepultura infidelis vel excommunicati post sententiam declaratoriam vel condemnatoriam.**

The quoted law clearly indicates that with the promulgation of the Code of Canon Law there are only four factors effecting the violation of a church. The wording of the preliminary portion of this law is so forceful that it excludes the possibility of the church becoming violated in any other way than by the commission of any one of the four acts that are specifically enumerated in the law. These four acts are given in the law not simply by way of illustration, but rather as constituting an exhaustive list of the causes that bring about the violation of a church.[21]

Before a church can become violated the law presupposes that the violative act must be: a) certain, that is, exclusive of all reasonable

[17] Cf. Vermeersch-Creusen, *Epitome*, II, n. 489; De Meester, *Compendium*, III, p. 36, nota 2.

[18] C. un., *de consecratione ecclesiae vel altaris*, III, 21, in VI°.

[19] Canon 1207.

[20] Canon 1172, § 2.

[21] Cf. Beste, *Introductio in Codicem*, p. 564.

doubt; b) notorious either in law or in fact; c) committed in the church itself. These three conditions must be present in each case, otherwise the violation and its consequences do not ensue. A fuller consideration will be given to each of these conditions after a study of the factors which effect the violation of a church has been made.

Article I. Factors Effecting Violation

A. *Crime of Homicide*

As in the pre-Code legislation, so, likewise, under the present law of the Code, the violation of a church is induced by the commission of homicide therein. Homicide must be strictly understood as the killing of any human being. Attempted homicide which is not fatal does not violate the church in which it was committed, regardless of the seriousness of the injuries sustained by the victim. In the latter case, however, the church may be violated perhaps by reason of an unjust and grave shedding of blood.[22]

It is immaterial whether the death of a person is procured by poison, strangulation, or the use of a weapon.[23]

Before the violation of a church can be effected it must necessarily be presupposed that the homicide committed therein was a crime.[24] The very nature of a crime presupposes that the transgression of a law is morally imputable to the delinquent.[25] It follows, then, that the homicide must be voluntary and unjust, that is, the crime must be committed deliberately and involve serious sin.[26] Hence, an accidental killing caused, for example, by some falling object would not induce any violation of the church in which it occurred. Neither

[22] Cf. canon 1172, § 1, 2°.

[23] Cf. Gasparri, *De Ssma. Eucharistia*, n. 250; Coronata, *De Locis et Temporibus Sacris*, n. 28, 1°, a; Ayrinhac, *Administrative Law*, p. 21; Augustine, *A Commentary*, VI, 36.

[24] Canon 1172, § 1, 1°: "Delicto homicidii." For the penalties imposed upon those who are guilty of the crime of homicide cf. canon 2354.

[25] Cf. canon 2195, § 1.

[26] Cf. Gasparri, *De Ssma. Eucharistia*, n. 250; De Meester, *Compendium*, n. 1132, 2°; Many, *De Locis Sacris*, n. 31; Schmalzgrueber, *Ius Ecclesiasticum Universum*, lib. III, tit. 40, n. 78; Reiffenstuel, *Ius Canonicum Universum*, lib. III, tit. 40, n. 19.

would a church be violated if homicide were committed by one who is morally irresponsible for his actions, e.g., by an infant or by an insane person.[27] If homicide were committed in a church by a person who was under the influence of an intoxicant or an opiate, the violation of the church would depend upon whether or not the agent foresaw his action; if the homicide had not been foreseen in any way, the violation of the church would not ensue, for under such circumstances the homicide could not be deemed to have been committed deliberately.[28]

It has been noted that the violation of a church is effected when the homicide committed therein is not only deliberate, but also unjust. Thus, if a person were attacked in a church and could not save his life except by killing the unjust aggressor, such an action would be justifiable, and the church would not be thereby violated.[29]

Prior to the Code it was the common opinion of the canonists that a church became violated when the execution of a just sentence of capital punishment occurred therein. The reason for the ensuing violation was that such an execution was not unjust to the condemned man, but it was unjust by reason of the sacredness of the place in which it occurred.[30] Augustine still adheres to the opinion of the pre-Code authors.[31] Such a view, however, must be rejected, for the execution of a capital sentence performed by the lawful authorities, even though it is not in keeping with the decorum or the sacredness of the place in which it occurs, nevertheless is a just killing, and therefore cannot be called a crime of homicide.[32] Whether such an execution would cause the violation of a church

[27] Bouuaert-Simenon, *Manuale Juris Canonici*, III, n. 17; De Meester, *loc. cit.*; Many, *loc. cit.*

[28] Cf. Gasparri, *loc. cit.*; Augustine, *A Commentary*, VI, p. 37; Reiffenstuel, *loc. cit.*; Barbosa, *De Officio et Potestate Episcopi*, pars II, alleg. 28, n. 5.

[29] Woywod, "The Law of the Church on Sacred Places"—*HPR*, XXV (1925), p. 1083; De Meester, *loc. cit.*; Bouuaert-Simenon, *loc. cit.*; Many, *loc. cit.*; Reiffenstuel, *loc. cit.*

[30] Pirhing, *Ius Canonicum*, lib. III, tit. 40, n. 10; Barbosa, *ibid.*, n. 25; Many, *loc. cit.*; Reiffenstuel, *loc. cit.*

[31] *A Commentary*, VI, 37.

[32] Cf. Feldhaus, *Oratories*, p. 91; Ayrinhac, *Administrative Law*, p. 21.

by reason of the fact that the church might thereby be subjected to impious or sordid uses will be seen later.

A strict interpretation of the word "homicide" does not include suicide, nevertheless a morally imputable act of suicide is generally accepted by the modern authors as being a factor which causes the violation of the church in which it is perpetrated.[33] The reason for departing from the strict interpretation in this instance is that the old law, which also used the word "homicide," was understood by the pre-Code canonists as including suicide.[34] Hence, according to the general principles of interpretation, the present law of the Code is to be understood in accordance with the interpretation given to the old law by the approved authors.[35]

The violation of a church does not ensue unless the injury that was inflicted in the church was the direct and proximate cause of death.[36] Thus, for example, if a person were seriously wounded in a church, but his death ultimately followed from pneumonia or some other illness that was contracted as the result of the infliction of the wound, there probably would be no violation of the church, because in this instance the inflicted injury was only an indirect and mediate cause of death.

The question arises whether violation occurs when a person is killed in a church as the result of a bombing in time of war. Before attempting to reply to the question at hand, it is necessary to understand the fundamental principals of the morality of killing in time of war. When all other means for effecting a peaceful settlement between nations have failed, war is permissible for the purpose of defending the rights of a nation and of its citizens against attack, or it is permissible for the purpose of vindicating the rights

[33] Vermeersch-Creusen, *Epitome*, II, n. 489; Coronata, *De Locis et Temporibus Sacris*, n. 28, 1°, a; Beste, *Introductio in Codicem*, p. 564; De Meester, *Compendium*, n. 1132, 2°, a; Bouuaert-Simenon, *Manuale Juris Canonici*, III, n. 17.

[34] Cf. Schmalzgrueber, *Ius Canonicum Universum*, lib. III, tit. 40, n. 79; Reiffenstuel, *loc. cit.*; Wernz, *Ius Decretalium*, III, n. 442; Gasparri, *De Ssma. Eucharistia*, n. 250; Many, *loc. cit.*

[35] Cf. canon 6, 2°.

[36] Gasparri, *loc. cit.*

that have been infringed upon or unjustly taken away. In order to attain this end it is permissible for a nation to use all the necessary means, provided that the employed means are not immoral by reason of the natural law and are not forbidden by international law. Thus the killing or wounding of the combatants and those who are actively engaged in the progress of the war is justifiable. It is likewise justifiable to destroy fortified cities, places of shelter for the fighting forces, etc. Non-combatants, however, such as children, women, the aged and the wounded and all others who are in no way actively engaged in the prosecution of the war, all have the status of innocent parties to the struggle; hence, the deliberate killing or wounding of these is intrinsically immoral. Likewise it is not morally justifiable to destroy property that possesses no military value and is not devoted in any way to aid the war effort.[37] By an application of these principals to the case of the bombing of a church and the subsequent killing of the persons within it, it is evident that if the church were used as a place of shelter for the combatants, no violation would occur, because the killing of the soldiers would be justifiable, and as such the homicide could not be considered a crime. If, however, a church as a sacred place of worship were deliberately bombed for the sake of killing the worshippers therein, such an action would violate the church, for the homicide would be both deliberate and unjust. On the other hand, if the bombing and killing were accidental, the violation of the church would not ensue. Since it would be difficult, however, to ascertain whether the bombing of a church was deliberate or accidental, the violation would be doubtful.[38]

The crime of homicide violates a church when the subject is actually killed in the church. An act is considered to have taken place in a church when it has its effect therein, as in the case of the victim

[37] Cf. Noldin-Schmitt, *Summa Theologiae Moralis iuxta Codicem Iuris Canonici* (21. ed., 3 vols., Oeniponte: Pustet, 1932), II, n. 352; Vermeersch, *Theologiae Moralis Principia, Responsa, Consilia* (2. ed., 4 vols., Brugis: Firme Charles Beyaert, 1926-1928), II, n. 637.

[38] Cf. Mahoney, "Reconciliation of Bombed Church"—*The Clergy Review*, XXI (1941), 116-117, where consideration is given only to an accidental bombing.

receiving a fatal wound in the church while the aggressor fired from the outside; but if the murderer fired from the church and killed a person in the street, there would be no violation, for the act in this case is to be considered as having occurred outside the church.[39] If, however, a person were seriously injured in a church and then death resulted elsewhere, the church would be none the less violated, because the actual killing was perpetrated in the church. On the other hand, if he were injured outside the church, and death followed within the church, no violation would ensue, because it was simply a death, and not the crime of homicide, that occurred in the church.[40]

B. *Unjust and Grave Shedding of Blood*

The law regarding the violation of a church which results from bloodshed occurring therein was contained in the decretals of Gregory IX [41] and of Boniface VIII.[42] The expression that was employed in the decretals to designate the factor effecting the violation of a church was "*effusione sanguinis,*" without any further qualification. According to the interpretation of the pre-Code canonists the shedding of blood had to be caused unjustly, and the blood that was shed had to be a considerable amount. These two concepts were incorporated into the enactment of the law of the Code which rules: "*Ecclesia violatur . . . iniuriosa et gravi effusione sanguinis.*"[43] To obtain a clear idea of the meaning of the present law, therefore, it will be necessary to have recourse to the interpretation given to the old law by the pre-Code authors.

The shedding of a small amount of blood does not cause the violation of a church. According to the pre-Code authors the word "*effusio*" signified a flow of blood. They contended that the shedding of a few drops was not sufficient to bring about the violation

[39] Coronata, *De Locis et Temporibus Sacris*, n. 28, 2°, c; Many, *De Locis Sacris*, n. 31; Barbosa, *Ius Ecclesiasticum Universum*, lib. II, cap. 4, n. 21.

[40] Barbosa, *ibid.*, n. 20; Many, *loc. cit.*; Reiffenstuel, *Ius Canonicum Universum*, lib. III, tit. 40, n. 19.

[41] C. 10, X, *de consecratione ecclesiae vel altaris*, III, 40.

[42] C. un., *de consecratione ecclesiae vel altaris*, III, 21, in VI°.

[43] Canon 1172, § 1, 2°.

of a church. When referring to the amount that was required by law to bring about such an effect, the authors employed such terms as considerable, notable, abundant and copious flow of blood.[44] The expression "*gravi effusione*" of the present law is to be understood as conveying the same idea as that which was expressed by the pre-Code writers, namely, that the violation of a church is caused by the shedding of a considerable quantity of blood therein.

The shedding of blood alone, however, does not induce violation. The violation of a church ensues when the act that caused bloodshed was injurious or unjust, that is, the act itself was committed deliberately and was a serious transgression of the rights of another, so that the agent is reputed to have committed a gravely sinful act. Thus an accidental shedding of blood, or that which is caused by one who is devoid of the use of reason, does not induce violation.[45] Neither does the violation ensue when an effusion of blood is caused by a person who in self-defense justifiably inflicts a serious injury upon an unjust aggressor.[46] That the shedding of *human* blood alone is referred to in the law is evident from the use of the word *iniuriosa* or unjust. An animal cannot be a subject of rights (*subiectum iuris*); hence, the wounding of an animal and the subsequent shedding of blood would not be unjust, and consequently such bloodshed would not violate the church in which it occurred.[47]

It has been noted that a copious shedding of blood violates a church when the act that causes the bloodshed is grieviously sinful. Thus a fight between young boys, or a justifiable parental punishment of a child, which would occasion a considerable nose bleeding could not be considered to be a gravely sinful act, insofar as the

[44] Cf. *Glossa* in c. un., *de consecratione ecclesiae vel altaris,* III, 21, in VI°, v. "Nota primo"; Pirhing, *Ius Canonicum,* lib. III, tit. 40, n. 11; Barbosa, *De Officio et Potestate Episcopi,* pars II, alleg. 28, n. 34; Schmalzgrueber, *Ius Ecclesiasticum Universum,* lib. III, tit. 40, n. 80; Reiffenstuel, *Ius Canonicum Universum,* lib. III, tit. 40, n. 17.

[45] Schmalzgrueber, *loc. cit.;* Reiffenstuel, *ibid.,* n. 15.

[46] *Glossa* in c. un., *de consecratione ecclesiae vel altaris,* III, 21, in VI°, v. "sanguinis"; Reiffenstuel, *loc. cit.*

[47] *Glossa, ibid.,* v. "sanguinis humani"; Barbosa, *ibid.,* n. 31; Reiffenstuel, *loc. cit.;* Schmalzgrueber, *loc. cit.*

nose is a very sensitive organ, and a slight blow received upon the nose can very easily cause a great flow of blood.[48] It has been officially declared that a church is not violated even though a considerable amount of blood were shed as the result of a slight blow received upon the nose.[49] On the other hand, if a bleeding of the nose were caused by violent blows such as are inflicted by grown men, or by boys of fourteen or more years of age, the violation of the church would follow, for such an act is to be considered grievously sinful.[50]

Vermeersch-Creusen [51] and Coronata [52] are of the opinion that the serious wounding of a person is not "unjust" when such wounds are self-inflicted. They hold, therefore, that bloodshed which is caused by self-inflicted wounds in an attempt to commit suicide does not violate a church. Strictly taken, no one can commit an injustice against himself, for an injustice is a transgression against the rights of another. But man does not have dominion over his life; the supreme dominion over the life of a human being belongs to God alone, the Author of life. Therefore, a suicide attempted by the self-infliction of wounds is a transgression against the rights of God.[53] The shedding of blood that is caused by self-inflicted wounds, therefore, is unjust. It seems to follow, then, that bloodshed which is caused in this manner induces the violation of the church in which it takes place.

Before the violation of a church can be effected it is necessary that the unjust shedding of blood should be caused in the church. Thus if a person were wounded in the street, but the ensuing flow

[48] Pirhing, *Ius Canonicum*, lib. III, tit. 40, n. 11; Suarez, *Opera Omnia*, tract. *de eucharistia*, disp. LXXXI, sect. 4, n. 2; Barbosa, *ibid*., n. 36; Gasparri, *De Ssma. Eucharistia*, n. 251.

[49] S.C.C., in *Marsorum*, 18 dec. 1649—Pallottini, v. "ecclesia in genere," § III, n. 4. Twenty-four drops of blood was the amount of blood specifically mentioned in this decree.

[50] Barbosa, *loc. cit.*; Reiffenstuel, *ibid*., n. 16.

[51] *Epitome*, II, n. 489.

[52] *Institutiones Iuris Canonici*, n. 748, b.

[53] Cf. S. Thomas Aquinas, *Summa Theologica* (5 vols., Taurini, Italia: Marietti, 1932, IIª IIªᵉ, q. 64, art. 5; Noldin-Schmitt, *Theologia Moralis*, II, n. 326.

of blood took place in the church into which the victim fled, no violation would result.[54] Some authors claim that the infliction of a wound in a church causes the violation even though the subsequent flow of blood would occur elsewhere.[55] According to the strict interpretation of the law, however, the violation of a church is effected when both the cause of bloodshed and the actual flow of blood occurs therein.[56] The fact that the blood is absorbed by the person's clothing and does not come in contact with the church in any way does not make any difference.[57]

As has been explained under the heading of homicide, if a person is seriously wounded in a church while the malefactor was in the street, the violation nevertheless results, for the act is considered to have had its effect in the church even though it originated outside. There is no violation, however, if the victim is wounded outside the church even though the action of the aggressor originated in the church.

C. *Impious or Sordid Uses*

Canon 1172, § 1, 3°: [Ecclesia violatur] impiis vel sordidis usibus, quibus ecclesia addicta fuerit,

The third factor which induces violation is the subjecting of a church to impious or sordid uses. This provision of the law of the Code had no strict equivalent in the former legislation. The precise nature of the uses to which a church may not be subjected is not specified in the Code, but any sinful or disrespectful use that is unbecoming to the dignity and honor due to a sacred place of divine worship violates the church.

Canon 1178 rules that business transactions and fairs, even though held for a pious purpose, and in general all things that are not com-

[54] Reiffenstuel, *Ius Canonicum Universum*, lib. III, tit. 40, n. 18.

[55] Reiffenstuel, *loc. cit.*; De Meester, *Compendium*, n. 1132, 2°, b; Barin, "Commentarium"—*Ephemerides Liturgicae*, XXXVIII (1924), 236; Beste, *Introductio in Codicem*, p. 565.

[56] Cf. Vermeersch-Creusen, *Epitome*, II, n. 489; Barbosa, *De Officio et Potestate Episcopi*, pars II, alleg. 28, n. 24; Schmalzgrueber, *Ius Ecclesiasticum Universum*, lib. III, tit. 40, n. 80.

[57] Schmalzgrueber, *loc. cit.*; Barbosa, *loc. cit.*

patible with the sanctity of the place are forbidden in a church. Although the obligation to refrain from using a church for secular purposes is very strict, such uses would not induce violation, provided the uses were not impious or sordid.

The word "impious" has many meanings: irreligious, ungodly, sacrilegious, etc. Impious uses denote actions that are unlawful not only because they are objectively sinful, but also because they indicate disrespect for the sanctity of the church in which they are perpetrated.[58] Such uses would be the orgies that occurred in the Cathedral of Notre Dame during the French Revolution, or the so-called "Black Mass" in which the Sacred Host is profaned in the most outrageous manner.

Sordid uses are those actions that are neither sinful nor dishonorable in themselves, but are considered to be despicable and vile because of the grave irreverence that is manifested for the sacredness of the place in which they occur.[59] Thus, for example, a church would be violated if it were used as a place for the stabling of animals.

The word "*usus*" implies the necessity of an act being customary, or repeated, or at least continued for some length of time.[60] Bouuaert-Simenon are of the opinion that the subjecting of a church to impious or sordid uses for a day or two would induce violation,[61] while Coronata holds that violation would result if the church were used for several hours for such purposes.[62] It would be difficult to determine a definite minimum of time insofar as the performance of various actions with their accompanying circumstances are of unequal duration; but a single and brief impious or sordid act probably

[58] Cf. Beste, *Introductio in Codicem*, p. 563; Vermeersch-Creusen, *Epitome*, II, n. 489.

[59] Cf. Barin, "Commentarium" — *Ephemerides Liturgicae*, XXXVIII (1924), 236.

[60] Coronata, *De Locis et Temporibus Sacris*, n. 28, 1°, c; De Meester, *Compendium*, n. 1132, 2°, c; Beste, *loc. cit.*; Cocchi, *Commentarium in Codicem Iuris Canonici* (5 vols. in 8, Taurinorum Augustae: Marietti, 1922-1930), III, partes 2 et 3 (2. ed., *De Rebus*, 1926), n. 17 (hereafter this work will be referred to as *Commentarium*).

[61] *Manuale*, III, n. 17.

[62] *Institutiones Iuris Canonici*, n. 748, b.

would not cause the violation of the church. Thus, for example, the *effusio seminis* of the pre-Code discipline no longer induces violation, except in a case wherein such an act would recur frequently and become notorious. But this would be very unlikely unless the church were used as a brothel.[63]

It is generally admitted by the majority of the authors that a sacrilegious theft does not violate the church in which it is committed, for such an act ordinarily is very brief and the thief does not actually use the church.[64]

Relative to the infliction of capital punishment, referred to under the heading of homicide, Feldhaus denies that the use of the church for such a purpose would cause violation.[65] The more common and the more probable opinion, however, affirms that violation would be induced by the commission of an act of this kind,[66] for it can be reasonably presupposed that an official of the state who deliberately selects a church for the execution of a just sentence of capital punishment would be acting in contempt for religion with complete disregard for the decorum that is due a sacred place.

The Holy See has officially pronounced for the absolute exclusion from churches of all, even pious, theatrical performances and cinematographic projections.[67] Such plays and motion pictures, however, do not cause the violation of a church, for they cannot be considered either impious or sordid. On the other hand, however, violation would ensue if a church were used for an indecent theatrical presentation, a circus, a market place, or any other type of boisterous revelry.[68]

[63] Cf. Coronata, *Institutiones Iuris Canonici*, n. 748, b; Augustine, *A Commentary*, VI, 36; Cocchi, *loc. cit.*; O'Donnell, "Sacred Places and Sacred Times in the Code"—*Irish Ecclesiastical Record*, 5th series, XIII (1919), 460.

[64] Augustine (*op. cit.*, VI, 38) holds the opposite opinion.

[65] *Oratories*, p. 92.

[66] Vermeersch-Creusen, *Epitome*, II, n. 489; Cocchi, *loc. cit.*; Ayrinhac, *Administrative Law*, p. 22; De Meester, *loc. cit.*; Beste, *loc. cit.*

[67] S. C. Consistorialis, *Decretum circa actiones scenicas in ecclesiis*, 10 dec. 1912—AAS, IV (1912), 724.

[68] Cf. De Meester, *loc. cit.*; Beste, *loc. cit.*; Coronata, *De Locis et Temporibus Sacris*, n. 28, 1°, c.

Some authors maintain that a church is violated when it is used for the purpose of military barracks,[69] while others are of the opinion that violation ensues when the church is occupied by soldiers and also serves as a place to quarter horses and mules.[70] These opinions are based upon the pre-Code decisions of the Sacred Congregation of Rites. In one instance in which a church had been used in time of war to serve as barracks for soldiers and as a military point of observation for two days, it was declared that the church was to be reconciled provisionally (*ad cautelam*).[71] Reconciliation was demanded in another case in which several churches had been temporarily used as barracks for soldiers and as places of shelter for horses.[72] Under the law of the Code a church would be violated if it were used for the purpose of stabling animals of any kind, for such a purpose is most certainly to be considered sordid. But the temporary use of a church as living quarters for soldiers in time of war, particularly when other facilities are not available, would not cause violation, provided that there was no irreverence on the part of the occupants towards the sacredness of the church. The Church is forever solicitous about the temporal, as well as the spiritual, welfare of her children and is not opposed to the temporary use of a church as a place of shelter for those who, in time of war or other calamity, are deprived of their homes.[73]

It is held by some authors that a church is violated when it is used for heretical or schismatic religious services.[74] It is known, however, that the Holy See, by way of exception, tolerated a practice that existed for about three centuries in certain parts of Germany, namely, of holding Catholic and Protestant services in the

[69] Coronata, *De Locis et Temporibus Sacris*, *loc. cit.*; De Meester, *loc. cit.*; Beste, *loc. cit.*

[70] Augustine, *A Commentary*, VI, 38; Bouuaert-Simenon, *Manuale*, III, n. 17.

[71] S.R.C., *Tolentina*, 27 feb. 1847—*Decr. Auth.*, n. 2938.

[72] S.R.C., *Carpen.*, 3 mart. 1821—*Decr. Auth.*, n. 2612.

[73] Cf. Bouuaert-Simenon, *loc. cit.*; De Meester, *loc. cit.*

[74] De Meester. *loc. cit.*; Cocchi, *Commentarium*, III, partes 2 et 3, n. 17; Beste, *loc. cit.*

same church.[75] Although the use of a church for non-Catholic services can no longer be tolerated, it seems that no violation would ensue if it were used for such purposes, except in the case wherein the church was so used in contempt for the Catholic religion.[76]

D. *Burial of an Infidel or of a Person Excommunicated upon a Declaratory or a Condemnatory Sentence*

Canon 1172, § 1, 4°: [Ecclesia violatur] sepultura infidelis vel excommunicati post sententiam declaratoriam vel condemnatoriam.

The word "*sepultura*" is to be here understood only as the actual interment or entombment of a corpse. This is evident from canon 1175, which demands the removal or exhumation of the body of the person whose burial in the church caused the violation thereof. The other elements in connection with an ecclesiastical burial as enumerated in canon 1204 (the transfer of the body to the church and the funeral services in the church) are neither required nor do they alone suffice to cause violation.

Although the violation of a church is caused by the burial therein of an infidel or of a person excommunicated by declaratory or condemnatory sentence,[77] this does not imply that all other persons may be buried there. Canon 1205, § 2, forbids the burial in churches of all persons except residential bishops, abbots or prelates *nullius* in their own churches, or the Roman Pontiff, royal personages and Cardinals. Moreover, there is the possibility that some individuals

[75] Cf. Wernz, *Ius Decretalium*, III, scholion ad n. 447; Bargilliat, *Praelectiones Iuris Canonici*, II, n. 1420, e.

[76] Vermeersch-Creusen, *Epitome*, II, p. 337, nota 1; Bouuaert-Simenon, *ibid.*, n. 21.

[77] A condemnatory sentence is one in which a competent ecclesiastical judge inflicts the penalty of law. In a declaratory sentence, the law itself has already inflicted the penalty immediately when a crime has been committed, and the competent ecclesiastical judge merely declares that the delinquent has been found guilty, and that therefore he has incurred the penalty of the law. Cf. Woywod, *A Practical Commentary on the Code of Canon Law* (5. ed., 2 vols., New York: Wagner, 1939), I, 22.

or members of certain families have been granted a privilege by the Holy See whereby they are entitled to burial in a church. In view of the general norm given in canon 4 such privileges are not revoked by the law contained in canon 1205, § 2.[78]

The term "infidels" must be limited to persons who have never been baptized. The violation of a church results from the burial therein of unbaptized persons alone.

In the pre-Code law it was not certain that the burial of an infidel violated a church, insofar as there was no explicit legislation to that effect. It became customary, however, on the basis of some spurious decrees of Gratian, to consider those churches to be violated in which infidels had been buried.[79] Some of the pre-Code authors made an exception in favor of catechumens and unbaptized infants of Christian parents, maintaining that they were not, in the strict terminology of the law, included under the term "infidels." [80] Concerning the catechumens who die without receiving baptism through no fault of their own, canon 1239, § 2, confirms the opinion of the pre-Code authors by ruling that, in the matter of burial, they are to be considered equivalent to baptized persons. Hence, the burial of a catechumen in a church does not induce violation. Although the Code makes a specific exception for catechumens, it makes no concession for unbaptized infants of Christian parents. On the contrary, it rules generally, in the same canon that makes the exception for catechumens, that persons who die without first having received baptism are to be deprived of Christian burial.[81] It seems to follow that insofar as all unbaptized persons are infidels, their burial in a church would cause the violation thereof.[82] Most of the modern

[78] Canon 4: ". . . privilegia . . . quae, ab Apostolica Sede ad haec usque tempora personis sive physicis sive moralibus concessa, in usu adhuc sunt nec revocata, integra manent, nisi huius Codicis canonibus expresse revocentur."

[79] Cc. 27, 28, D. I, *de cons.;* cf. *supra,* p. 38.

[80] Gasparri, De *Ssm̃a. Eucharistia,* n. 253; Many, *De Locis Sacris,* n. 34, 3°; Schmalzgrueber, *Ius Ecclesiasticum Universum,* lib. III, tit. 40, nn. 72, 74.

[81] Canon 1239, § 1.

[82] Reiffenstuel, *Ius Canonicum Universum,* lib. III, tit. 40, n. 21; Suarez, *Opera Omnia,* tract. *de eucharistia,* disp. LXXXI, sect. 4, n. 6; S. Alphonsus de Ligorio, *Theologia Moralis,* lib. VI, n. 366; D'Annibale, *Theologia Moralis,*

canonists, however, following the more benign interpretation of the pre-Code authors, are of the opinion that the burial of an unbaptized infant of Christian parents does not induce violation. They maintain that such persons are not infidels in the strict sense of the term, insofar as they are not wilful infidels.[83] The opinion of these authors is not devoid of probability in view of the large number and the authority of those who hold it. However, in view of the fact that the ruling of the Code is couched in general terms, there seems to be no legal basis for making a distinction whereby the unbaptized infants of Christian parents should be excluded from the general ruling of the Code.

Concerning the violation of a church resulting from the burial therein of an excommunicated person, it was the common opinion of the pre-Code authors that violation was not caused unless the excommunicated person had been a *vitandus*. According to a Constitution of Pope Martin V an excommunicated person was to be considered a *vitandus* only when a judicial sentence to that effect had been published, or when a person was publicly and expressly denounced as such, or when the person was a notorious persecutor of the clergy.[84] In accordance with the law now in force no excommunicated person is a *vitandus*, unless he is by name excommunicated by the Apostolic See, unless the excommunication has been publicly announced, and unless in the decree or sentence it is expressly stated that he is a *vitandus*.[85] The Code makes one exception to the general rule. Persons who lay violent hands on the person of the Roman Pontiff become *excommunicati vitandi* by the very fact of having committed the crime.[86]

III, p. 15, nota 19; Woywod, "The Law of the Church on Sacred Places"—*HPR*, XXV (1925), 1085.

[83] Vermeersch-Creusen, *Epitome*, II, n. 489; De Meester, *Compendium*, n. 1132, 2°, d; cf. also Coronata, *De Locis et Temporibus Sacris*, n. 28, 1°, c; Beste, *Introductio in Codicem*, p. 565; Feldhaus, *Oratories*, p. 92; Augustine, *A Commentary*, VI, 38.

[84] Martinus V (in Conc. Constantien.), const. "*Ad evitanda*," anno 1418—*Fontes*, n. 45; Mansi, XVII, 1192-1193.

[85] Canon 2258, § 2.

[86] Canon 2343, § 1, 1°.

The law now in force rules that the burial of an excommunicated person causes the violation of a church when the excommunication has been pronounced by a declaratory or by a condemnatory sentence. Some authors claim that the meaning of the present law is the same as that of the pre-Code law, the difference being merely verbal.[87] Coronata, in an early work,[88] limited the violation of a church to the burial therein of a *vitandus* who was excommunicated by condemnatory or declaratory sentence. In a later work [89] he seemed to retract his earlier view, and held that it was not necessary that the excommunicated person be a *vitandus*, but that the violation of a church was induced by the burial therein of any excommunicated person against whom a declaratory or condemnatory sentence of excommunication had been passed.[90]

Excommunicated persons are either *vitandi* or *tolerati*.[91] Insofar as canon 1172, § 1, 4°, does not specify either of the two, it seems that the burial of either type causes the violation of a church, provided that a declaratory or condemnatory sentence has been given. The reason why some authors hold that a church is violated by the burial therein of a *vitandus*, and not of a *toleratus*, whose excommunication was inflicted by the sentence of a competent ecclesiastical authority, is that canon 1242 creates some difficulty by the fact that, following upon the enumeration of persons who are forbidden to be honored with Christian burial,[92] it provides only for the removal of the bodies of *excommunicati vitandi* from a Christian burial place. Likewise, canon 1175, which provides for the removal of an excommunicated person buried in a church, does not qualify the type of excommunication, but states simply that, if the church

[87] Blat, *Commentarium*, III, partes II-VI, n. 22; O'Donnell, "Sacred Places and Sacred Times in the Code"—*Irish Ecclesiastical Record*, 5th series, XIII (1919), 460.

[88] *De Locis et Temporibus Sacris*, n. 28, 1°, c.

[89] *Institutiones Iuris Canonici*, n. 748, b.

[90] Cf. also Vermeersch-Creusen, *Epitome*, II, n. 489; Bouuaert-Simenon, *Manuale*, III, n. 17; De Meester, *Compendium*, n. 1132, 2°, d; Beste, *Introductio in Codicem*, p. 565; Ayrinhac, *Administrative Law*, p. 33; Augustine, *A Commentary*, VI, 39.

[91] Canon 2258, § 1.

[92] Cf. Canon 1240.

has been violated by the burial of an excommunicated person, the body is to be removed from the church before the rite of reconciliation is performed.[93] It seems that the text of canon 1172, § 1, 4°, which rules that a church is violated by the burial of a person excommunicated upon a declaratory or condemnatory sentence, is clear, and that it cannot be limited only to *excommunicati vitandi* without making a gratuitous addition to the specification of the Code. Canon 1175 evidently refers to canon 1172, § 1, 4°, when it rules that the body of an excommunicated person, by whose burial the church was violated, is to be removed before reconciliation. Rossi [94] points out that the reason why canon 1242 insists only on the removal of an *excommunicatus vitandus* from a cemetery, and not of the other persons excommunicated by sentence of an ecclesiastical judge, is that the Church is more severe in reference to burial in a church. This reason, however, is only partially satisfactory. A legal and more satisfactory reason is provided in canon 1207, which rules that the laws governing the violation and reconciliation of churches are to be applied also to cemeteries. Therefore, insofar as canon 1175 rules that the bodies of infidels and excommunicated persons are to be removed from a church before the rite of reconciliation is performed, by virtue of canon 1207 such bodies are also to be removed from a cemetery. Canon 1242, therefore, provides for the removal of the bodies of the *excommunicati vitandi,* and canons 1175 and 1207 provide for the removal of all other bodies that caused the violation of a cemetery.

Canon 2343, § 1, 1°, rules that those who lay violent hands on the person of the Roman Pontiff become *excommunicati vitandi.* This penalty is incurred by the very fact of one's having committed the crime. The penalty is inflicted by the law itself, and there is no necessity of issuing a declaratory or condemnatory sentence of excommunication. The question, then, arises whether violation ensues as the result of the burial of such a person in a church. Vermeersch-Creusen maintain that the church is violated if in it such

[93] Cf. Coronata, *De Locis et Temporibus Sacris,* p. 29, nota 1.

[94] *La "Sepultura Ecclesiastica" e L' "Ius Funerum" nel Diritto Canonico* (Bergamo: Libreria Vescovile Editrice Mario Arnoldi, 1920), p. 52, footnote.

a person is buried, because canon 1242 demands the exhumation of the body of an *excommunicatus vitandus* which has been interred in a sacred place.[95] It must be admitted that canon 1242 demands the exhumation of the bodies of all *excommunicati vitandi*, but it does not regulate that the burial of one who has been so penalized by the law itself induces violation. Canon 1172, § 1, 4°, states explicitly that a church is violated by the burial therein of an *excommunicated person against whom a condemnatory or declaratory sentence of excommunication has been passed.* Therefore, in view of the express wording of this canon, it seems to be contrary to the law to hold that violation results from the burial of an *excommunicatus vitandus* against whom no sentence has been pronounced. In like manner heretics, schismatics and apostates from the faith are not included in the category of excommunicated persons whose burial would violate a church, unless a condemnatory or declaratory sentence of excommunication has been issued against them by a competent ecclesiastical judge.[96]

Article II. Requisite Conditions for Violation

It has been pointed out that the commission of any one of the acts specified in law and described above causes the church to become violated. The law, however, rules further that the acts must be certain, notorious, and committed in the church itself. These conditions are of such importance that the law does not consider a church to be violated if any one of the three is not verified.

A. *Certainty Regarding the Committed Act*

Certainty implies that the violative acts are committed under such circumstances as to exclude all doubt whether of law or of fact. A doubt of law is one in which there is no certainty about the existence, the extent, or the application of the law. Relative to the existence of the law, there can be no doubt, for the law concerning the vio-

[95] *Epitome*, II, n. 489.

[96] Cf. Augustine, *A Commentary*, VI, 39; Woywod, "The Law of the Church on Sacred Places"—*HPR*, XXV (1925), 1086.

lation of churches is expressly stated in the Code. There may be a doubt, however, concerning the extent or the application of the law to a particular case in question. Thus, for example, there may be a doubt about what amount of the shedding of blood must be presupposed before the violation of a church takes place by reason of bloodshed that is unjustly caused therein.[97] A doubt of fact arises when the law itself is clear, but when there is no certainty concerning the existence of the fact or of the circumstances of the fact. Thus, for example, in the case of suicide committed in the church by an insane person who has lucid intervals, it would be uncertain whether the person was morally responsible for his actions when he killed himself .

When an objective doubt cannot be solved, there can be no establishment of certainty. Hence the commission of a violative act which remains doubtful either in law or in fact causes the violation to be doubtful. There is no obligation of performing the rite of reconciliation when the violation of a church is doubtful, but a provisional (*ad cautelam*) reconciliation may take place.[98]

B. Notoriety Regarding the Committed Act

Another condition required by law before the violation of a church ensues is that the committed act must be notorious. An act may be notorious by notoriety of law or by notoriety of fact. It is notorious by law when sentence has been pronounced by a competent judge in a civil or ecclesiastical trial,[99] or after a confession has been made in court by the agent either spontaneously or in answer to a legitimate question proposed by the judge.[100] An act is factually notorious when it is publicly known and committed under such circumstances that it cannot be concealed by any subterfuge or excused by any counteractive remedy at law.[101] In other words, the fact of the commission of the act and the culpability of the agent must be publicly known. According to these legal definitions, therefore, it may be pointed out that an act is notorious

97 Cf. Augustine, *A Commentary*, VI, 39.

98 Canon 1174, § 2.

99 Cf. Coronata, *Institutiones Iuris Canonici*, n. 1646.

100 Cf. canons 2197, 2° and 1750.

101 Cf. canon 2197, 3°.

when it is publicly known by the fact that it appears in public documents and legal and authentic records,[102] or that it is already widely publicized, commonly known, or certainly bound to become such. Some authors are of the opinion that at least six persons in a small community must know of the act before it can be considered to be publicly known, and more persons in proportion to the greater number of inhabitants in larger places. However, canonists also consider the quality or character of the persons who witnessed the act. Thus, for example, even if one talkative person witnessed the act, it would soon become widely publicized in view of the tendency of the individual to divulge what he has witnessed. On the other hand, if the commission of the act were witnessed by several prudent and discreet persons, who are not likely to divulge the fact, the act would remain occult.[103] In this latter case no violation would ensue, because of the lack of notoriety of the act. If, however, the commission of an act became publicly known at some later date, the church is considered to be violated from the time at which the fact became thus known.[104]

C. *Localization of the Committed Act in the Church Proper*

A third and final condition that must be verified before a church is legally considered to be violated is that the act must be committed within the church (*in ipsa ecclesia*). In ordinary usage the term "church" refers to the entire building, but its application in canon 1172, § 1, must be interpreted as meaning that part of the building in which divine services are held. An act committed within the interior limits of the walls of the church and in the space between the floor and the ceiling is an act of which it can be said that it is committed in the church. The sacristy is not a part of the church

[102] Cf. Coronata, *op. cit.*, IV, p. 15, n. 1646, nota 3; Blat, *Commentarium*, V, n. 9.

[103] Cf. Coronata, *op. cit.*, n. 1648; Vermeersch-Creusen, *Epitome*, III, n. 384, 3°; Ayrinhac-Lydon, *Penal Legislation in the New Code of Canon Law* (New York: Benziger Brothers, 1936), n. 6.

[104] Schmalzgrueber, *Ius Ecclesiasticum Universum*, lib. III, tit. 40, n. 82; Pirhing, *Ius Canonicum*, lib. III, tit. 40, n. 12; Reiffenstuel, *Ius Canonicum Universum*, lib. III, tit. 40, n. 22.

when the term "church" is understood in its proper meaning; neither is the vestibule or portico, nor are the adjoining buildings and rooms, nor the rooms in the tower, nor the space between the inside ceiling and the outside roof.[105]

A basement chapel or a basement burial place, to which there is direct access from the interior of the church proper, constitutes one unit with the church itself and consequently shares the consecration or the blessing of the church. Hence the commission of a violative act in such a basement violates the church. On the other hand, if such a basement is so constructed that accesss to it can be had only through an entrance outside of the church proper, it is a unit distinct from the church. Consequently, the violation of such a basement chapel or burial place does not involve the violation of the church, or vice versa.[106]

Burial crypts that are built into the walls or under the floor of a church are likewise considered to be part of the church itself, insofar as entrance to such places can be had only from the interior of the church. Consequently, when a violative act occurs in such a crypt the church itself is violated.[107]

[105] Beste, *Introductio in Codicem*, p. 564; Blat, *Commentarium*, III, partes II-VI, n. 22; De Meester, *Compendium*, n. 1132, 1°; Gasparri, *De Ssm̃a. Eucharistia*, n. 247; Pirhing, *Ius Canonicum*, lib. III, tit. 40, n. 16.

[106] De Meester, *loc. cit.*; Vermeersch-Creusen, *Epitome*, II, n. 489; Bouuaert-Simenon, *Manuale*, III, n. 17; Beste, *loc. cit.*; Many, *De Locis Sacris*, n. 38, 3°.

[107] Cf. Many, *loc. cit.*

CHAPTER VI

CONSEQUENCES OF THE VIOLATION OF CHURCHES

Canon 1173, § 1: In ecclesia violata, antequam reconcilietur, nefas est divina celebrare officia, Sacramenta ministrare, mortuos sepelire.

§ 2: Si violatio accidat tempore divinorum officiorum, haec statim cessent; si ante Missae canonem vel post communionem, Missa dimittatur, secus sacerdos Missam prosequatur usque ad communionem.

The consequences of the violation of a church are twofold: a) all divine services must cease; b) the church must be reconciled.

ARTICLE 1. CESSATION OF DIVINE SERVICES

It is unlawful to celebrate divine services in a violated church until reconciliation has taken place. Although the injunction is a grave one, no penalty either of censure or of irregularity is attached to the transgression. The reason for the prohibition, as Schmalzgrueber points out, is that in the moral judgment of man it is repugnant that before the place has been purified the Immaculate Host should be consecrated and the divine services celebrated in a place that has been defiled by evil deeds.[1] Divine services are defined in canon 2256, § 1, as those functions of the power of orders which by the institution of Christ or of the Church are ordained for divine worship and are performed exclusively by the clergy, such as the celebration of Mass, the administration of the sacraments, the conducting of funeral services, the ministry of preaching, the holding of sacred processions, etc. Pious devotions, on the other hand, such as the making of the stations of the cross, the recitation of the rosary and other forms of prayer and meditation, are non-liturgical functions, and are not considered to be divine services, even though a priest officiates at them.[2] The law, therefore, does not forbid the

[1] *Ius Ecclesiasticum Universum*, lib. III, tit. 40, n. 63.

[2] Hyland, *Excommunication, its Nature, Historical Development and Effects*, The Catholic University of America Canon Law Studies, n. 49 (Washington, D. C.: The Catholic University of America, 1928), p. 54.

exercise of such functions in a violated church. Some authors, however, claim that even non-liturgical functions may be forbidden, because the exercise of such functions in a violated church may be a source of scandal to the faithful.[3] The possibility of scandal and also of wonderment to the faithful may be avoided simply by means of an explanation to them that the exercise of non-liturgical functions is not prohibited in a violated church. The authors who hold the opposite opinion seem to read into the law a greater severity than the law itself contains.

The presumptuous transgression of the prohibition to celebrate divine services in a violated church involves grave moral imputability.[4] The authors are in agreement that when a grave cause is present, e. g., if there is no other church in which the faithful can fulfill their obligation of hearing Mass, and if in addition a reconciliation cannot be effected immediately, the ordinary may permit the celebration of Mass in a violated church. Likewise in a case of urgent necessity, e. g., if Mass must be celebrated for the purpose of supplying the needed presence of Holy Viaticum, and no other church is available, the permission of the ordinary for the celebration of Mass in a violated church may be presumed, if he cannot be reached.[5] It is to be noted, however, that if there is sufficient time for the actual performance of the rite of reconciliation, Mass may not be celebrated in the violated church, for canon 1176 grants very extensive faculties for effecting the prompt reconciliation of a violated church, as will be noted in the following chapter.

Vermeersch-Creusen point out that when Mass is celebrated in a violated church because of a grave cause or in view of an urgent necessity, care should be taken lest the faithful be scandalized by such an action. It is suggested that the faithful should be informed

[3] Barin, "Commentarium"—*Ephemerides Liturgicae*, XXXVIII (1924), 237; "De Ecclesia Violata"—*Promptuarium Canonico-Liturgicum*, as reviewed in *Jus Pontificium*, IX (1929), 170.

[4] D'Annibale, *Theologia Moralis*, III, n. 15; Schmalzgrueber, *Ius Ecclesiasticum Universum*, lib. III, tit. 40, n. 64.

[5] Coronata, *De Locis et Temporibus Sacris*, n. 29; De Meester, *Compendium*, n. 1133; Many, *De Locis Sacris*, n. 40, 5°; Gasparri, *De Ssma. Eucharistia*, n. 243; Wernz, *Ius Decretalium*, III, n. 443.

of the reason for postponing the reconciliation and also of the reason for allowing the celebration of Mass under such conditions.[6]

When the violation of a church happens during divine services, these must cease immediately. Thus, the general rubrics of the *Missal* prescribe that if during the celebration of Mass the violation occurs before the Canon, the Mass must be discontinued at once; if, however, the violation occurs after the Canon of the Mass has already begun, the Mass shall not be discontinued.[7] By virtue of the canon now under discussion the prescription of that rubric of the Missal must be corrected. The present ruling is that if the violation of a church occurs before the Canon of the Mass, or after the Communion, the Mass must be discontinued immediately; if it occurs between the Canon, i.e., beginning with the words "*Te igitur,*" and the Communion, the Mass is to be continued only as far as the Communion, i.e., until the "*Corpus tuum*" inclusively.[8]

The administration of the sacraments is likewise forbidden in a violated church. If the violation occurs during the administration of the sacraments, they must be discontinued at once. By analogy with the ruling concerning the continuance of Mass when the violation occurs during the celebration thereof, it seems that the administration of a sacrament should be discontinued immediately if the violation occurs during the prayers and ceremonies that precede or follow the actual administration of the sacrament; if the violation occurs during the essential ceremony of a sacrament, no interruption must take place until the rites necessary for the administration of that sacrament are completed, but the prayers and ceremonies that ordinarily would follow are to be omitted.[9] If the violation occurs during the administration of a sacrament that does not allow an interruption, the rite is to be continued to its completion.[10] This would be

[6] *Epitome*, II, n. 489.

[7] *Missale Romanum, tit. De defectibus in celebratione missarum occurrentibus*, c. X, *de defectibus in ministerio ipso occurrentibus*, n. 2: "Si, Sacerdote celebrante, violetur Ecclesia ante Canonem, dimittatur Missa; si post Canonem, non dimittatur."

[8] Canon 1173, § 2.

[9] Barin, "Commentarium"—*Ephemerides Liturgicae*, XXXVIII (1924), 237-238; Moretti, *De Sacris Functionibus*, I, n. 346.

[10] Beste, *Introductio in Codicem*, p. 566.

the case if violation took place while the sacrament of Penance was being administered. If the penitent had begun the confession of his sins before the violation took place, the confessor would have to pronounce the absolution if the penitent was worthy even though a violation had been committed in the interval.

Another divine service the celebration of which is expressly forbidden by law in a violated church is the burial of the dead (*In violata ecclesia . . . nefas est . . . mortuos sepelire*). The "burial of the dead" as understood here does not mean the interment of the dead in the church, but rather the obsequies or funeral services that are held in a church over the bodies of the faithful departed.[11] When the violation of a church occurs while a funeral service is being performed therein the service must be terminated immediately. If, however, the violation occurs during the celebration of the Mass of Requiem, the principles regarding the violation of a church occurring while Mass is being celebrated apply here in the same manner as has already been pointed out above.

Relative to the celebration of all other divine services the general ruling of the Code is that they may not be held in a violated church, and if the violation occurs during their celebration, they must immediately be stopped. Thus the public recitation of the canonical hours, preaching, sacred processions, and any other liturgical function must be brought to an end at once. If the Blessed Sacrament is exposed upon the altar for public adoration, It must be replaced in the tabernacle without the performance of any ceremony.[12]

When it can be foreseen that the violation of a church is to ensue, the Blessed Sacrament, the holy oils, the baptismal water, the relics of the saints and all other movable sacred objects are to be removed from the church. Such procedure is to be carried out particularly in time of an invasion, when there is danger of the church's being occupied by the invaders and subjected to impious and sordid uses; for under such circumstances there would be grave danger that the sacred things would become the object of contempt and even of profanation[13]

[11] Cf. Beste, *Introductio in Codicem*, p. 566; Vermeersch-Creusen, *Epitome*, II, n. 489.

[12] Moretti, *De Sacris Functionibus*, I, n. 346.

[13] Cf. Barin, "Commentarium"—*Ephemerides Liturgicae*, XXXVIII (1924),

It has been officially declared that the violation of a church does not entail the suspension or the withholding of the indulgences that can be gained by making a visit to the church.[14]

Article 2. Necessity of Reconciliation

Reconciliation is a sacred rite by which a violated church is restored to its pristine condition so that divine services may be celebrated again therein.[15]

A church which has been violated must be reconciled as soon as that is possible according to the rites prescribed in the approved liturgical books, i. e., in the *Roman Pontifical* and the *Roman Ritual*.[16] It has been officially declared that the saying of Mass in a violated church, e. g., in a case of necessity, does not dispense with the necessity of performing the rite of reconciliation.[17] The obligation of reconciling a violated church is a grave one, and therefore the blemish brought upon a church by violation must be effaced as quickly as possible. But there is an obligation only when the violation is certain;[18] if the violation is only doubtful, a provisional (*ad cautelam*) reconciliation may take place, but it is not obligatory.[19] If a provisional reconciliation were given to a church that was doubtfully violated, and later it became apparent that the violation was certain, it would not be necessary to reconcile the church again.[20]

A church which has become violated by the burial therein of an excommunicated person or of an infidel shall not be reconciled until after the body of that person has been removed from the church, if

238; *Promptuarium Canonico-Liturgicum*, "De Ecclesia Violata" as reviewed in *Jus Pontificium*, IX (1929), p. 170.

14 S. C. Indulg., 18 sept. 1862, *Ordinis Carmelitarum Discalceat.—Decreta Authentica S. C. Indulg.*, n. 396; *Fontes*, n. 5066.

15 Cf. Coronata, *De Locis et Temporibus Sacris*, n. 30, 1°; Cocchi, *Commentarium*, V, n. 19.

16 Canon 1174, § 1.

17 S.R.C., 19 aug. 1634, *Oppiden.*, ad II—*Decr. Auth.*, n. 611; *Coll. S.C. de Prop. Fide* (ed. 1907), n. 78.

18 Cf. canon 1172, § 1.

19 Cf. canon 1174, § 2.

20 Blat, *Commentarium*, III, pars II, n. 24; Coronata, *Institutiones Iuris Canonici*, n. 749, b.

the removal can be accomplished without grave inconvenience.[21] A grave inconvenience would exist in the case wherein there are many bodies buried in a church and the difficulty of distinguishing the remains of the infidel or of the excommunicated person would require the calling in of experts and witnesses, which may involve great expense. Under such circumstances the removal of the bodies would not be required.[22] Nor would the removal of the bodies be insisted upon in the case in which the civil authorities have an express prohibition against the removal of the remains of the dead from their final resting place. A breach of a civil law of this kind may involve a pecuniary penalty, imprisonment, or both.[23] The Church does not wish that any extraordinary encumbrance should be suffered in the observance of the ruling of this law. Hence, the legislator makes an exception when such unusual circumstances are present.

The question arises whether a violated church must be reconciled when the removal of the remains of an infidel or of an excommunicated person cannot be accomplished without grave inconvenience. It seems that the Code insists upon the reconciliation of the church, even though in view of rightfully acknowledged difficulties the body has not yet been removed. Regardless of whether or not the body has been removed, it is necessary to reconcile a violated church before the celebration of divine services may be permitted therein.[24]

[21] Canon 1175.

[22] Coronata, *ibid.*, c; Augustine, *A Commentary*, VI, 44.

[23] Cf. Coronata, *loc. cit.*

[24] Coronata, *loc. cit.;* Coronata, *Compendium Iuris Canonici* (2 vols., Taurini: Marietti, 1937-1938), n. 1273.

CHAPTER VII

RECONCILIATION OF VIOLATED CHURCHES

ARTICLE I. MINISTER

The liturgical rite of the reconciliation of a violated church distinguishes between a church which has been merely blessed and one which has been consecrated. Accordingly the minister who performs the rite of reconciliation of a consecrated church is distinct from the reconciling minister of a blessed church. The law of the Code is more liberal than the old law with regard to the persons who may reconcile a violated church. In the more extensive faculties of the new law, the Code to a large extent removes one of the principal objects that delayed the reconcilation of a violated church, and thereby renders its restoration for divine worship more easy of attainment.[1]

A. *Blessed Churches*

Prior to the Code the reconciliation of a blessed church was to be performed by the local ordinary or by a priest delegated by him.[2] A reconciliation which was performed by a priest without explicit delegation was valid, but illicit.

The present law of the Code declares:

> **Ecclesiam benedictam reconciliare potest rector eiusdem vel quilibet sacerdos de consensu saltem praesumpto rectoris.**[3]

The rector of a blessed church may reconcile it by his own authority.[4] The delegation of the local ordinary is no longer required

[1] Feldhaus, *Oratories*, p. 95.

[2] S. R.C., *Nolana*, 8 iulii 1904—*Decr. Auth.*, n. 3091; *Analecta Ecclesiastica*, XII (1904), 383; *ASS*, XXXVII (1904), 117; *Rituale Romanum* (ed. 1911), tit. VIII, cap. 28, *Ritus reconciliandi ecclesiam violatam*, n. 8.

[3] Canon 1176, § 1.

[4] The term "rector" is to be here understood as designating the person to whom the care of any church has been committed, and not in the restricted meaning given in canon 479, § 1.

by the Code or the *Roman Ritual*;[5] nor is the consent or the permission of the local ordinary necessary. Any other priest may also reconcile a blessed church with at least the presumed consent of the rector of the church. The consent of the rector may be presumed when he is absent and the necessity arises for the reconciliation of the church.[6] Any priest may lawfully presume the consent of the rector, unless he is absolutely forbidden by the latter, or is convinced of the intention of the rector to perform the rite himself.[7] If, however, a priest were to reconcile a blessed church when he was forbidden to do so by the rector of the church, the reconciliation nevertheless would be valid but illicit, for every priest by law is vested with the right to reconcile a blessed church. The exercise of that right is restricted unless the consent of the rector is given expressly, or, at least, presumptively.

B. *Consecrated Churches*

Prior to the Code the reconciliation of a consecrated church was a sacred rite the exercise of which was reserved exclusively to bishops, so that any cleric who lacked the episcopal power of orders could not validly reconcile a consecrated church unless he had obtained a special indult from the Holy See.[8]

The ruling of the Code is that the reconciliation of a consecrated church can be validly performed by those persons who have the right by law to bless sacred places.[9] Hence, the reconciliation of a consecrated church is to be performed by the local ordinary, if the church belongs to the secular clergy or to a non-exempt religious congregation or to a lay organization. If the church belongs to an exempt religious clerical body, the major superior has the right to reconcile it. But both the local ordinary and the major religious

[5] *Rituale Romanum* (ed. 1926), tit. VIII, cap. 28, *Ritus reconciliandi ecclesiam violatam*, n. 1.

[6] Coronata, *Institutiones Iuris Canonici*, n. 749, d.

[7] Augustine, *A Commentary*, VI, 44.

[8] C. 9, X, *de consecratione ecclesiae vel altaris*, III, 40; *Rituale Romanum* (ed. 1911), tit. VIII, cap. 28, *Ritus reconciliandi ecclesiam violatam*, n. 8.

[9] Canon 1176, § 2.

superior may delegate another priest to reconcile a consecrated church.[10]

The present law no longer requires that the minister of reconciliation of a consecrated church should be endowed with the episcopal character. Because the Code permits a major superior of an exempt religious clerical community and even a simple priest with the required delegated power to reconcile a consecrated church, it is apparent that the exercise of that liturgical rite is a sacerdotal function. Coronata claims that the reconciliation of a consecrated church would be valid if performed by a simple priest without delegation from his ordinary.[11] Barin,[12] De Meester,[13] Vermeersch-Creusen [14] and Bouuaert-Simenon,[15] on the other hand, are of the opinion that the reconciliation of a consecrated church which is performed by a simple priest without any delegation from his ordinary would be not only illicit but also invalid. This opinion seems to be the more probable one, for it is in complete harmony with the wording of the Code. The reconciliation of a consecrated church is reserved to the ordinary, but it may be delegated to another priest. Canon 1147, § 3, prescribes that a reserved blessing, when given by a priest without the necessary permission, is illicit but valid, unless in the reservation the Holy See has declared otherwise. In view of the ruling of this canon it may seem that the reconciliation of a church performed by a priest without delegation is indeed illicit but nevertheless valid. Canon 1176, § 2, however, states explicitly that the *valid* reconciliation of a consecrated church is to be performed by the ordinary or by a priest delegated by him. Therefore the reconciliation of a consecrated church which is performed by a simple priest without express delegation from his ordinary must be considered not only illicit but also invalid.

[10] Cf. canons 1176, § 2, and 1156. Henceforth when the term "ordinary" is used alone, it will designate the local ordinary and major superior of an exempt religious clerical community—cf. canon 198, § 1.

[11] *De Locis et Temporibus Sacris*, p. 32, nota 4; *Institutiones Iuris Canonici*, n. 749, d.

[12] "Commentarium"—*Ephemerides Liturgicae*, XXXVIII (1924), 281.

[13] *Compendium*, n. 1134, nota 1.

[14] *Epitome*, II, n. 490.

[15] *Manuale Juris Canonici*, III, n. 20

The Code provides further for extraordinary cases wherein the reconciliation of a consecrated church may be performed validly and licitly by a priest without delegation from his ordinary:

> **In casu tamen gravis et urgentis necessitatis, si Ordinarius adiri nequeat, rectori ecclesiae consecratae eandem reconciliare fas est, certiore facto postea Ordinario.**[16]

This liberal concession was entirely unheard of before the Code. It is the purpose of this unusual privilege to facilitate the possibility of reconciling a church without undue delay.

The right of reconciling a consecrated church, which is granted to its rector, can be applied only when the conditions stated in the law are verified, namely, serious and urgent necessity, and the impossibility of approaching the ordinary for the purpose of having him reconcile the church, or for the purpose of obtaining the required delegation to reconcile the church. If the rector of a consecrated church erred in his judgment concerning the existence of a serious and urgent necessity, and nevertheless reconciled the church, the reconciliation would not be invalid.[17]

A serious and urgent necessity would exist when the use of the church is required for divine services, e. g., for the celebration of Mass on Sundays and holy days so that the faithful may fulfill their obligation of hearing Mass; for the celebration of Mass on any day of the week for the purpose of consecrating the Holy Eucharist which is to be given as Viaticum to the dying; for the conducting of a funeral service; for the continuation of a mission, etc.

The impossibility of approaching the ordinary may arise by reason of the fact that his residence is far distant from the place where the violated church is situated, or by reason of the absence of the ordinary from his place of residence, or also in view of the impossibility of reaching him at the place of his sojourn.

The power of the rector to reconcile a consecrated church when the conditions stated in law are verified is granted to him by reason of his office. This power, then, is an ordinary power and can be

[16] Canon 1176, § 3

[17] Cf. Coronata, *Institutiones Iuris Canonici*, n. 749, d.

delegated, under the same circumstances, to another priest.[18] It is to be noted, however, that this delegation must be expressly made; the consent of the rector cannot be presumed as in the case of the reconciliation of a blessed church. In the case of grave and urgent necessity the delegation of the rector of the church is required for the validity of the reconciliation of a consecrated church, in the same manner as the delegation of the ordinary is required for the valid performance of that liturgical rite outside of the case of necessity.

The Code prescribes that, after the rector of a consecrated church uses the privilege which is granted to him by law, he shall notify the ordinary of this fact. Failure to notify the ordinary would not affect the validity of the reconciliation.[19] The purpose in notifying the ordinary is to make possible the entering of a record which will remove all doubt in the event that at some future date a question may arise concerning the actual performance of, or the validity of the performed, reconciliation.

Article II. Rites and Ceremonies

Canon 1177: Reconciliatio ecclesiae benedictae fieri potest aqua lustrali communi; reconciliatio vero ecclesiae consecratae fiat aqua ad hoc benedicta secundum leges liturgicas; quam tamen non solum Episcopi, sed etiam presbyteri qui ecclesiam reconciliant, benedicere possunt.

The rites and ceremonies of reconciliation of a blessed church must be taken from the *Rituale Romanum*.[20] The water which is to be used in the ceremony is ordinary holy water. The *Ritual* does not prescribe that the water should be blessed immediately preceding the ceremony; hence, water that had been previously blessed,

[18] Barin, "Commentarium"—*Ephemerides Liturgicae*, XXXVIII (1924), 281; Vermeersch-Creusen, *Epitome Iuris Canonici*, II, n. 490; Coronata, *De Locis et Temporibus Sacris*, n. 30, 3°, c.

[19] Coronata, *Institutiones Iuris Canonici*, n. 749, d.

[20] Tit. VIII, cap. 28, *Ritus reconciliandi ecclesiam violatam*.

as for example on the preceding Sunday before high Mass, may be used in the reconciliation of the church.

The ceremony consists of the sprinkling of the outside walls of the church with holy water, of the recitation of the Litany of the Saints, of several prayers before the altar, and of the sprinkling of the inside walls of the edifice. Holy water must also be sprinkled upon the place where the violative act was committed. The ceremony is concluded with the celebration of the Mass of the day.[21]

The rites and ceremonies which are to be employed in the reconciliation of a consecrated church must be taken from the *Pontificale Romanum,*[22] regardless of whether a bishop or a priest with the required delegation performs the ceremony.[23]

The water which is to be used for the reconciliation of a consecrated church is specially prepared with two distinct blessings. The first of these is the blessing of water with an admixture of a small amount of salt. This blessing of water constitutes a part of the ceremony of reconciliation and is to be performed before the principal door of the church. There follows a sprinkling of the exterior walls with the holy water, and the singing or recitation of the Litany of the Saints. Special holy water is then prepared, the blessing of which calls for the presence of salt, ashes and wine, which are mixed with the water.[24] With this blessed water the celebrant proceeds around the interior of the church three times, sprinkling the upper and lower parts of the walls as well as the floor, particularly the spot in which the violative act was committed. This part of the ceremony is followed by several prayers, a Preface, a psalm and the blessing of the people by the minister. The ceremony is concluded with the Mass of the day celebrated by the officiating minister or by another priest. In the Mass a special oration, noted in the Pontifical, is added to the oration of the feast of the day.

[21] *Rituale Romanum, ibid.*, n. 7.

[22] Pars II, *De Ecclesiae, et Coemeterii Reconciliatione.*

[23] *Rituale Romanum, ibid.*, n. 8.

[24] The ceremony for the blessing of this water is found in the *Pontificale Romanum,* Pars II, *De Ecclesiae Dedicatione seu Consecratione.* Prior to the Code a priest who with an apostolic indult reconciled a consecrated church could not perform the blessing of this water; the water had to be blessed by a bishop—cf. S.R.C., *Salamantina,* 12 dec. 1761—*Decr. Auth.*, n. 2463.

Chapter VIII

PENALTIES PROVIDED BY LAW AGAINST THOSE WHO CAUSE THE VIOLATION OF A CHURCH

Canon 2329: Ecclesiae . . . violatores, de quibus in can. 1172 . . . , interdicto ab ingressu ecclesiae aliisque congruis ab Ordinario pro gravitate delicti puniantur.

It has been pointed out in an earlier part of this work that at the time of the *Decretum* of Gratian and until the time of the Decretals of Gregory IX there was but a vague idea of the violation of churches as it is understood today.[1]

Prior to the Code there were no penalties specified in law that were to be applied to those who were guilty of a moral contamination or violation of a church. The above named sources, however, contained penalties for those who physically violated a church. This physical violation consisted of a violent breaking into or spoliation of a church or other sacred places.[2] There is evidence that as early as the late fifth century there existed penal legislation against those who committed acts which were then considered to effect the violation of a church. Pope Gelasius (492-496) in a letter to one Epiphanus directed that a kind of personal interdict be imposed by bishops on those who violated churches.[3] Gratian repeated this prescription in his *Decretum,*[4] and also included among his canons one that prescribed excommunication for those who caused the violation of churches.[5] There is, moreover, evidence that by the time of the

[1] Cf. *supra*, pp. 30-31.

[2] Cf. Wernz, *Ius Decretalium*, VI, n. 409.

[3] "Ad episcopos ceteres dereximus iussionem, ut eos, qui ecclesias violasse perhibentur, accessu earum iudicent esse indignos."—Jaffé, *Regesta Romanorum Pontificum*, n. 446.

[4] Cf. c. 11, C. XVII, q. 4.

[5] "Canonica instituta et sanctorum patrum exempla sequentes, ecclesiarum Dei violatores auctoritate Dei et iudicio sancti Spiritus a gremio sanctae matris ecclesiae et a consortio totius Christianitatis eliminamus, quodusque resipis-

Decretals of Gregory IX excommunication was the ecclesiastical penalty for those who caused the violation of churches, for that Pontiff ruled that any Christian who was cut off from communion with the Church for this crime could be absolved when he was in danger of death and was not to be denied Christian burial or the suffrages of the Church.[6] The decretals indicated that the excommunication was imposed as a *latae sententiae* censure on those who caused the violation of a church,[7] but all such penalties were abrogated in the Constitution *Apostolicae Sedis,* issued by Pope Pius IX, for in that document the Supreme Pontiff ruled that all *latae sententiae* penalties not specifically mentioned in the above-cited Constitution were null and void. Certainly there was no mention in the document concerning any penalty for the violation of churches.[8] Between the time of the promulgation of the Constitution *Apostolicae Sedis* in 1869 and the advent of the Code, however, those who violated churches could be excommunicated by means of a *ferendae sententiae* or even a *latae sententiae* through particular law.[9]

Some canonists, moreover, advocated that those who were guilty of such violations but refused to make adequate satisfaction should be denied absolution and if they persisted in their impenitence should be denied Christian burial.[10]

The present law is definitely different from the penal prescriptions of the pre-Code discipline. Canon 2329 rules that those who cause a church to be violated by the acts listed in canon 1172 must

cant et ecclesiae Dei satisfaciant."—C. 107, C. XI, q. 3. (The origin of this legislation cannot be determined.)

[6] "Parochiano tuo, qui excommunicatus pro manifestis excessibus, videlicet, homicidio, incendio, violenta manuum iniectione in personas ecclesiasticas, ecclesiarum violatione vel incestu fuit, dum ageret in extremis, per presbyterum suum iuxta formam ecclesiae absolutus, non debent coemeterium et alia ecclesiae suffragia denegari, sed eius heredes et propinqui, ad quos bona pervenerunt ipsius, ut pro eodem satisfaciant, censura sunt ecclesiastica compellendi."—C. 14, X, *de sepulturis,* III, 28.

[7] Cf. Wernz, *loc. cit.;* c. 22, X, *de sententia excommunicationis,* V, 39; c. 21, § 1, C. XVII, q. 4.

[8] Cf. *Fontes,* n. 552.

[9] Cf. Wernz, loc. cit.

[10] Cf. Wernz, *loc. cit.*

be punished by the ordinary with an interdict forbidding them to enter a church. Besides this punishment there are also prescribed other penalties proportionate to the gravity of the crime. It has been pointed out that a church may be violated by the crime of homicide, by an unjust and grave shedding of blood, by the subjecting of a church to impious or sordid uses, and by the burial therein of an infidel or of one who was excommunicated upon a declaratory or condemnatory sentence.[11]

The Code aptly places the delict of the violation of a church among those crimes which are listed as militating against religion. The violation of a church is in reality a sacrilege, an unworthy treatment of a sacred thing which is dedicated to God by public authority. It is for this reason that the crime is an offense against religion.[12]

It is to be noted that canon 2329 speaks of those who cause the violation of a *church*. The latter term, therefore, is to be understood in the sense of canon 1161,[13] which defines a church as a sacred building dedicated to divine worship, principally for the purpose that it may be used by all the faithful for the public exercise of divine worship. Canon 2329, therefore, is not to be understood in such a manner as to include also the violators of an oratory, which is defined by the Code as a place destined for divine worship, not however with the principal object of serving the faithful at large for public worship.[14] This opinion is in harmony with the principles of the interpretation of penalties as given in canon 2219, § 3, which rules that there must be no extending of a penalty from one case to another.[15] For analogy is not admitted in interpreting penal laws, even if the reasons or circumstances of persons and cases are quite alike.[16] Hence, because of the difference between a church and a

[11] Cf. canon 1172, § 1.

[12] Cf. Chelodi, *Ius Poenale* (4. ed., Tridenti: Libreria Moderna Editrice A. Ardesi, 1935), p. 87.

[13] Cf. Blat, *Commentarium*, V *(De Delictis et Poenis)*, n. 168.

[14] Cf. canon 1188, § 1.

[15] "Non licet poenam de persona ad personam vel de casu ad casum producere, quamvis par sit ratio, imo gravior, salvo tamen praescripto can. 2231."

[16] Cf. Augustine, *A Commentary*, VIII (3 ed., St. Louis: Herder, 1931), p. 80.

public oratory, the penalty prescribed for the violator of a church cannot be said to apply also to the violator of an oratory. Had the legislator wished to include both types of violation under the same penalty, it would have been noted in the law.

This is not to be interpreted, of course, as meaning that the violator of an oratory cannot be punished. The Code provides that a superior may penalize a transgressor, even though there is no sanction of law against the crime he has committed, if there be scandal given or if the special gravity of the transgression demands that punishment be inflicted.[17]

There can be no doubt that the Code establishes a *ferendae sententiae* penalty for those who cause the violation of a church. Since the penalty prescribed must be now *inflicted* by the ordinary,[18] the present law in this respect is greatly different from the old, which prescribed a *latae sententiae* penalty for those who physically violated a church. Until the time of the Constitution *Apostolicae Sedis* of Pope Pius IX a transgressor was excommunicated by the very fact of a willful physical violation of a church and no judicial sentence was necessary for the effects of that punishment to result therefrom. According to the present law, the penalties provided by law do not come into effect until they are inflicted by the ordinary.

It must be noted that the Code uses the word "ordinary" in designating the one who must inflict the penalties of law on those who are guilty of the violation of a church. This term must be understood in the light of canon 198, § 1, which also includes as ordinaries the major superiors in clerical exempt religious communities for their subjects. In any violation of a church, therefore, by a member of an exempt clerical community, the major superior properly inflicts the penalties prescribed by law.

Although the vicar general is by law included under the term

[17] Canon 2222, § 1: "Licet lex nullam sanctionem appositam habeat, legitimus tamen Superior potest illius transgressionem, etiam sine praevia poenae comminatione, aliqua iusta poena punire, si scandalum forte datum aut specialis transgressionis gravitas id ferat. . . ."

[18] Cf. canon 2217, § 1, 2°; Augustine, *A Commentary*, VIII, 319; Coronata, *Institutiones*, n. 1918; Vermeersch-Creusen, *Epitome*, III, n. 528; Blat, *Commentarium*, V, n. 168.

"ordinary," he is, according to the prescriptions of the Code, without power to inflict the penalties of law on those who are guilty of the violation of a church, unless he has a special mandate from the episcopal ordinary.[19]

The penalties provided by law against those who are guilty of the crime of violating a church—interdict *ab ingressu ecclesiae* and other penalties proportionate to the gravity of the crime—are stated preceptively by the Code,[20] which means that the ordinary is not entirely free to inflict or not to inflict them. The Code legislates as follows for those cases in which the law uses preceptive words in prescribing penalties:

The penalty of law is ordinarily to be imposed, but it is left to the conscience and discretion of the judge or superior:

1) to delay the imposition of the penalty to a more opportune time, if it is judged that greater evils may follow from a hasty punishment of the delinquent;

2) to refrain from inflicting the penalty if the delinquent has shown complete amendment and has repaired the scandal, or if he has been or will be sufficiently punished by the civil authorities;

3) to moderate a specific penalty or to employ instead some penal remedy or penance, if there is some circumstance which considerably diminishes his liability, or if, though the offender has amended or has been sufficiently punished by the civil authorities, the judge or superior deems it advisable to add some mild punishment.[21]

The punishment to be inflicted on the one who causes the violation of a church is an interdict from entering a church. Now this punishment is in the nature of a personal particular interdict,[22] but the Code seems to distinguish between a strictly personal interdict and an interdict from entering a church.[23] An interdict *ab ingressu ecclesiae* is a mild type of personal interdict which does not entail

[19] Canon 2230, § 2: "Vicarius Generalis sine mandato speciali non habet potestatem infligendi poenas."

[20] Cf. Augustine, *loc. cit.;* Coronata, *loc. cit.*

[21] Cf. canon 2223, § 3, 1°, 2°, 3°.

[22] Cf. Woywod, *A Practical Commentary on the New Code of Canon Law*, II, 448.

[23] Compare canons 2275 and 2277.

all of the prohibitions of canon 2275 which are imposed on those who are under a strict personal interdict, nor does it have any effect outside of a church.[24]

Canon 2277 rules that an interdict *ab ingressu ecclesiae* entails the prohibition to celebrate divine services in a church, to assist at them, and to receive ecclesiastical burial; if the person so interdicted nevertheless assists, he need not be expelled, and, if he is buried, the body need not be exhumed. The term "church" is to be understood according to canon 1161, so that a person interdicted *ab ingressu ecclesiae* is not forbidden to celebrate or assist at divine services in an oratory.[25]

Woywod holds that the prohibition to assist at divine services in a church implies also the prohibition to receive the sacraments in a church.[26] The more common opinion, however, holds that a person interdicted *ab ingressu ecclesiae* may enter a church for the purpose of private prayer and also for the private reception of the Sacraments.[27] This opinion seems to be more probable than that of Woywod, for canon 2275, which governs the effects of personal interdict, prohibits the celebration and assistance at divine services and specifically adds the prohibition of the reception of the sacraments. Insofar as this latter prohibition is specifically mentioned in canon 2275, and no such provision is made in canon 2277, it seems that the reception of the sacraments in a church is not to be forbidden to one who is interdicted *ab ingressu ecclesiae*.

The ecclesiastical burial, which is prohibited, is to be understood in the sense of canon 1204, that is, as denoting the transfer of the body to the church, the funeral services in the church and the interment in a place legitimately appointed for the burial of the

[24] Cf. Vermeersch-Creusen, *Epitome*, III, n. 478; Cappello, *De Censuris iuxta Codicem Iuris Canonici* (3. ed., Taurinorum Augustae: Marietti, 1933), n. 472; Ayrinhac, *Penal Legislation*, n. 141.

[25] Cappello, *loc. cit.;* Ayrinhac, *loc. cit.;* Coronata, *Institutiones Iuris Canonici*, n. 1797; Woywod, *A Practical Commentary*, II, 449.

[26] *Loc. cit.*

[27] Beste, *Introductio in Codicem*, p. 922; Coronata, *loc. cit.;* Cappello, *loc. cit.*

faithful departed.[28] Hence, no funeral rite whatsoever is to be performed in the church. If, however, contrary to the prescriptions of the law such an interdicted person is buried in a church (i. e., if he is one of those mentioned in canon 1205 who would ordinarily be privileged to receive burial in a church), or in a cemetery, there is no legal obligation to exhume or remove the body from its burial place.

In addition to the interdict *ab ingressu ecclesiae* canon 2329 provides that other congruous penalties are to be inflicted by the ordinary on those who cause the violation of a church. Unless the ameliorating prescriptions of canon 2223, § 3, can be followed, the ordinary must inflict the penalties, for the wording of the law is preceptive. Such a penalty may comprise the compensation for the expenses incurred by repairing the damages that the church may have suffered when it was violated, or the recitation of specified prayers, the observance of a special fast, the making of a pious pilgrimage, the giving of alms for a worthy cause, and other similar works of piety or of religion.[29]

[28] Cf. Coronata, *loc. cit.*
[29] Cf. canon 2313, § 1.

CONCLUSIONS

1. The desecration of a church by the destruction of a major part of the walls results only when the major part of the walls is in a state of ruins at one given period of time, and not when small portions are destroyed successively and at diverse times. (Cf. pp. 53-55).

2. The local ordinary may licitly reduce a church to a secular status and purpose even though the conditions of canon 1187 are not verified, provided some other just cause exists. (Cf. pp. 62-64).

3. The vicar general cannot reduce a church to a secular status and purpose unless he has a special mandate. (Cf. p. 58).

4. The term "infidel" as employed in canon 1172, § 1, 4°, is to be understood as referring to all unbaptized persons; consequently, the burial of such a person in a church induces the violation thereof. (Cf. pp. 81-82).

5. There can be no violation of a church by the burial therein of an *excommunicatus vitandus* against whom no condemnatory or declaratory sentence of excommunication has been given. (Cf. pp. 83-85).

6. The penalties of canon 2329, which are to be inflicted upon persons who are guilty of violating a church, are not to be applied to those who violate an oratory. (Cf. pp. 103-104).

BIBLIOGRAPHY

Sources

Acta Apostolicae Sedis, Commentarium Officiale, Romae: 1909-

Acta Sanctae Sedis, 41 vols., Romae: 1865-1909.

Acta et Decreta Sacrorum Conciliorum Recentiorum, Collectio Lacensis, 7 vols., Friburgi Brisgoviae: 1870-1890.

Canones et Decreta Concilii Tridentini, ed. novissima, Romae: Typographia polyglotta S. C. de Prop. Fide, 1882.

Codex Iuris Canonici Pii X Pontificis Maximi iussu digestus, Benedicti Papae XV auctoritate promulgatus, Romae: Typis Polyglottis Vaticanis, 1933.

Codicis Iuris Canonici Fontes cura Emi. Petri Card. Gasparri editi, 9 vols., Romae (postea Civitate Vaticana): Typis Polyglottis Vaticanis, 1923-1939. (Vols. VII-IX, ed. cura et studio Emi. Iustiniani Card. Serédi.)

Collectanea S. Congregationis de Propaganda Fide seu Decreta, Instructiones, Rescripta pro Apostolicis Missionibus ex Tabulario eiusdem Sacrae Congregationis deprompta, Romae: 1893.

Collectanea S. Congregationis de Propaganda Fide seu Decreta, Instructiones, Rescripta pro Apostolicis Missionibus, 2 vol., Romae: 1907.

Corpus Iuris Canonici, ed. Lipsiensis 2, post Aemilii Ludovici Richteri curas instruxit Aemilius Friedberg, 2 vols., Lipsiae: Tauchnitz, 1879-1881, editio anastatice repetita, Lipsiae: 1928.

Decreta Authentica Congregationis Sacrorum Rituum ex Actis eiusdem collecta eiusque auctoritate promulgata sub auspiciis SS. D.N. Leonis Papae XIII, 6 vols., Romae: 1898-1927.

Decreta Authentica Sacrae Congregationis Indulgentiis Sacrisque Reliquiis praepositae ab anno 1668 ad annum 1882 edita iussu et auctoritate SS. D.N. Leonis PP. XIII, Ratisbonae: 1883.

Decretales D. Gregorii IX, una cum Glossis Restitutae, Romae: 1582.

Decretum Gratiani Emendatum et notationibus illustratum una cum Glossis, Gregorii XIII, Pont. Max. iussu editum, 2 vols., Romae: 1582.

Gardellini, Aloisius, *Decreta Authentica Congregationis Sacrorum Rituum ex actis eiusdem collecta*, 3. ed., 4 vols., cum appendicibus, Romae: 1856-1887.

Hardouin, Jean, *Acta Conciliorum et Epistolae Decretales ac Constitutiones Summorum Pontificum*, 12 vols., Parisiis: 1715.

Jaffé, Philippus, *Regesta Pontificum Romanorum ab condita Ecclesia ad annum post Christum natum MCXCVIII*, ed. 2., 2 vols., in 1, correctam et auctam auspiciis Gulielmi Wattenbach curaverunt S. Loewenfeld, F. Kaltenbrunner, P. Ewald, Lipsiae: 1885-1888.

Liber Sextus Decretalium D. Bonifacii Papae VIII suae integritati una cum Clementinis et Extravagantibus earumque Glossis restitutis, Romae: 1582.

Mansi, Ioannes Dominicus, *Sacrorum Conciliorum Nova et Amplissima Collectio*, 53 vols. in 59, Paris-Arnhem-Leipzig: 1901-1927.

Missale Romanum ex decreto Sacrosancti Concilii Tridentini restitutum S. Pii V Pontificis Maximi iussu editum aliorum Pontificum cura recognitum a Pio X reformatum et Ssmi. D.N. Benedicti XV auctoritate vulgatum, Ratisbonae: Sumptibus et Typis Friderici Pustet, 1924.

Pallottini, S., *Collectio Omnium Conclusionum et Resolutionum Quae in causis propositis apud Sacram Congregationem Cardinalium S. Concilii Tridentini interpretum prodierunt ab eius institutione anno MDLXIV ad MDCCCLX, distinctis titulis alphabetico ordine per materias digestas,* 17 vols., Romae: 1868-1895.

Pontificale Romanum Summorum Pontificum iussu editum a Benedicto XIV et Leone XIII Pontificibus Maximis recognitum et castigatum, Ratisbonae, Neo-Eboraci et Cincinnati: Pustet, 1891.

Rituale Romanum Pauli V Pontificis Maximi iussu editum a Benedicto XIV auctum et castigatum cui novissima accedit Benedictionum et Instructionum Appendix, Romae, Tornaci: Typis Societatis S. Ioannis Evangelistae, 1911.

Rituale Romanum Pauli V Pontificis Maximi iussu editum aliorumque Pontificum cura recognitum atque auctoritate Ssmi. D.N. Pii Papae XI ad normam Codicis Juris Canonici accomodatum, Taurini-Romae: Marietti, 1926.

Thesaurus Resolutionum Sacrae Congregationis Concilii, 167 vols., Romae: 1718-1908.

Wilkins, D., *Concilia Magnae Brittaniae et Hiberniae,* 4 vols., Londini: 1737.

Reference Works

Aquinas, S. Thomas, *Summa Theologica,* 5 vols., Taurini (Italia): Marietti, 1932.

Augustinus, Antonius, *Antiquae decretalium collectiones commentariis et emendationibus illustratae,* Parisiis: 1621.

Ayrinhac, H. A., *Administrative Legislation in the New Code of Canon Law,* New York: Longmans, Green & Co., 1930.

Ayrinhac, H. A.-Lydon, P. J., *Penal Legislation in the New Code of Canon Law,* New York: Benziger Brothers, 1936.

[Bachofen], Charles Augustine, *A Commentary on the New Code of Canon Law,* 8 vols., St. Louis: Herder. (Vol. VI, *Administrative Law,* 3. ed., 1931; Vol. VIII, *Penal Code,* 3. ed., 1931.)

Barbosa, Augustinus, *Iuris Ecclesiastici Universi Libri Tres,* Lugduni: 1660.

Barbosa, Augustinus, *Pastoralis Solicitudinis sive De Officio et Potestate Episcopi Tripartita Descriptio,* Lugduni: 1656.

Bargilliat, M., *Praelectiones Juris Canonici,* 25. ed., 2 vols., Parisiis: 1909.

Benedictus XIV, *De Synodo Dioecesana,* 3 vols., Romae: 1778.

Berardi, Carolus, *Gratiani Canones Genuini ab Apocryphis Discreti, Corrupti ad emendationem Codicum Fidem Exacti, Difficiliores Commoda Interpretatione Illustrati,* 4 vols., Venetiis: 1777.

Beste, Udalricus, *Introductio in Codicem*, Collegeville, Minn.: St. John's Abbey Press, 1938.

Bingham, Joseph, *The Antiquities of the Christian Church*, 2 vols., London: 1856.

Blat, Albertus, *Commentarium Textus Codicis Iuris Canonici*, 5 vols. in 6, Romae: ex typographia pontificia in instituto Pii IX, 1921-1927.

Bliley, Nicholas Martin, *Altars According to the Code of Canon Law*, The Catholic University of America Canon Law Studies, n. 38, Washington, D. C.: The Catholic University of America, 1927.

Bouuaert, F. Claeys-Simenon, G., *Manuale Juris Canonici*, 3 vols., Gandae et Leodii: H. Dessain, 1930-1931; Vol. III, 3. ed., 1931.

Cappello, Felix M., *De Censuris iuxta Codicem Iuris Canonici*, 3. ed., Taurinorum Augustae: Marietti, 1933.

Cappello, Felix M., *Tractatus Canonico-Moralis de Sacramentis*, 3 vols. in 6, Taurinorum Augustae: Marietti, 1932-1939. (Vol. I, *De Sacramentis in genere, de Baptismo, Confirmatione et Eucharistia*, 3. ed., 1938.)

Chelodi, Ioannes, *Ius Poenale et Ordo Procedendi in Iudiciis Criminalibus iuxta Codicem Iuris Canonici*, 4. ed., Tridenti: Libreria Moderna Editrice A. Ardesi, 1935.

Cocchi, Guidus, *Commentarium in Codicem Iuris Canonici*, 5 vols. in 8, Taurinorum Augustae: Marietti, 1922-1930. (Vol. III, partes II et III, *De Rebus*, 2. ed., 1926.)

Coronata, Matthaeus Conte a, *Compendium Iuris Canonici*, 2 vols., Taurini (Italia): ex Officina Libraria Marietti, 1937-1938.

Coronata, Matthaeus Conte a, *De Locis et Temporibus Sacris*, Taurinorum Augustae: Marietti, 1922.

Coronata, Matthaeus Conte a, *Institutiones Iuris Canonici*, 5 vols., Taurini (Italia): ex Officina Libraria Marietti, 1933-1939. (Vol. II, *De Rebus*, 2. ed., 1939; Vol. IV, *De Poenis et Delictis*, 1935.)

Cicognani, Amleto G., *Canon Law*, 2. ed., Philadelphia: Dolphin Press, 1935.

D'Annibale, Iosephus, *Summula Theologiae Moralis*, 5. ed., 3 vols., Romae: 1908.

De Angelis, Philippus, *Praelectiones Iuris Canonici ad Methodum Decretalium Gregorii IX Exactae*, 4 vols., in 6, Romae: 1877-1887.

De Ligorio, S. Alphonsus M., *Theologia Moralis*, 2 vols., Augustae Taurinorum: 1891.

De Meester, A., *Juris Canonici et Juris Canonico-Civilis Compendium*, nova ed., 3 vols. in 4, Brugis: Desclée de Brouwer et S[i]., 1921-1928.

De Rossi, G. B., *La Roma Sotterranea Cristiana*, 3 vols., Roma: 1864-1877.

De Rozière, Eugene, *Liber Diurnus ou Recueil des Formules usitées par la Chancellerie Pontificale du Ve au XIe siécle*, Paris: 1869.

Duchesne, L., *Christian Worship, Its Origin and Evolution*, 5. ed., London: MacMillan Co., 1931.

Feldhaus, Aloysius H., *Oratories*, The Catholic University of America Canon

Law Studies, n. 42, Washington, D. C.: The Catholic University of America, 1927.

Ferraria, Sigismund, *Bullarium seu Collectio Bullarum et Litterarum Apostolicarum*, 6 vols., Romae: 1640-1650.

Ferraris, F. Lucius, *Prompta Bibliotheca, Canonica, Juridica, Moralis, Theologica, necnon Ascetica, Polemica, Rubricistica, Historica*, ed. Migne, 8 vols., Parisiis: 1860-1863.

Gasparri, Petrus, *Tractatus Canonibus de Sanctissima Eucharistia*, 2 vols., Parisiis et Lugduni: 1897.

Gonzalez-Tellez, Manuel, *Commentaria Perpetua in singulos textus Quinque Libros Decretalium Gregorii IX*, 5 vols. in 4, Venetiis: 1699.

Hinschius, Paulus, *Das Kirchenrecht der Katholiken und Protestanten in Deutschland*, 6 vols., Berlin: 1869-1897. Vols. I-IV, *System des Katholischen Kirchenrechts*, Berlin: 1869-1888.

Hinschius, Paulus, *Decretales Pseudo-Isidorianae et Capitula Angilramni*, Lipsiae: 1863.

Hyland, Francis E., *Excommunication, Its Nature, Historical Development and Effects*, The Catholic University of America Canon Law Studies, n. 49, Washington, D. C.: The Catholic University of America, 1928.

Lindsay, W. M., *Isidori Hispalensis Episcopi Etymologiarum sive Originum Libri XX*, 2 vols. in 1, Oxonii, 1911.

Migne, Jacques Paul, *Patrologiae Cursus Completus, Series Latina*, 221 vols., Parisiis: 1844-1864.

Migne, Jacques Paul, *Patrologiae Cursus Completus, Series Graeca*, 161 vols., Parisiis: 1856-1866.

Moretii, Aloisius, *Caeremoniale iuxta Ritum Romanum seu De Sacris Functionibus*, 4 vols., Taurini (Italia): Marietti, 1936-1939.

Muratori, Ludovicus A., *Liturgia Romana Vetus*, 2 vols., Venetiis: 1748.

Noldin, H.—Schmitt, A., *Summa Theologiae Moralis iuxta Codicem Iuris Canonici*, 21. ed., 3 vols., Oeniponte: Pustet, 1932.

Ojetti, Benedictus, *Synopsis Rerum Moralium et Iuris Pontificii*, Romae: 1899.

Panormitanus (Nicholaus de Tudeschis), *Commentaria in Quinque Libros Decretalium*, 5 vols. in 7, Venetiis: 1588.

Pirhing, Ernricus, *Ius Canonicum Nova Methodo Explicatum, omnibus capitulis titulorum promiscue et confuse positis in ordinem doctrinae digestis*, 5 vols. in 4, Dilingae: 1674-1678.

Reiffenstuel, Anacletus, *Ius Canonicum Universum*, 5 vols. in 7, Parisiis: 1864-1882.

Rossi, Giuseppe, *La "Sepultura Ecclesiastica" e L'"Ius Funerum" nel Diritto Canonico*, Bergamo: Libreria Vescovile Editrice Mario Arnoldi, 1920.

Sanchez, Thomas, *De Sancto Matrimonii Sacramento Disputationum Libri Tres*, Venetiis: 1614.

Santi, Franciscus, *Praelectiones Iuris Canonici*, 4 vols. in 2, Ratisbonae: 1886.

Scherer, Rudolph von, *Handbuch des Kirchenrechts*, 2 vols., Graz und Leipzig: 1886-1898.

Schmalzgrueber, Franciscus, *Ius Ecclesiasticum Universum*, 5 vols. in 12, Romae: 1843-1845.

Schroeder, H. J., *Disciplinary Decrees of the General Councils*, St. Louis: Herder, 1937.

Schulte, A. J., *Benedicenda*, New York-Cincinnati-Chicago: 1907.

Schulte, Joh. Friedrich von, *Die Summa des Stephanus Tornacensis uber das Decretum Gratiani*, Giessen: 1891.

Schuster, Ildefonso, *The Sacramentary (Liber Sacramentorum)*, translated from the Italian by Arthur Levelis-Marke, M.A., 5 vols., London: Burns, Oates & Washbourne, Ltd., 1924.

Singer, Heinrich, *Die Summa Decretorum des Magister Rufinus*, Paderborn: 1902.

Smith, William—Cheetham, Samuel, *A Dictionary of Christian Antiquities*, 2 vols., Hartford: 1880.

Suarez, Franciscus, *Opera Omnia*, 26 vols., Parisiis: 1856-1866.

Thesaurus Linguae Latinae, Lipsiae: 1900—

Van Hove, A., *Commentarium Lovaniense in Codicem Iuris Canonici*, Vol. I, Tom. I, *Prolegomena*, Mechliniae-Romae: H. Dessain, 1928.

Vermeersch, A., *Theologiae Moralis Principia, Responsa, Consilia*, 2. ed., 4 vols., Brugis: Firme Charles Beyaert, 1926-1928.

Vermeersch, A.—Creusen, J., *Epitome Iuris Canonici*, 3 vols., Mechlinae-Romae: H. Dessain, 1934-1937. (Vol. I, ed. 6., 1937; Vols. II et III, ed. 5., 1934-1936.)

Waterworth, J., *The Canons and Decrees of the Sacred and Oecumenical Council of Trent*, London: 1849.

Wernz, Franciscus X., *Ius Decretalium*, 6 vols. in 10, Romae et Prati: 1905-1914. (Vol. III, pars II, ed. 2., *De Rebus*, 1908; Vol. VI, *Ius Poenale*, 1913.)

Wernz, Franciscus X.—Vidal, Petrus, *Ius Canonicum*, 7 vols. in 8, Romae: apud Aedes Universitatis Gregorianae, 1923-1938.

Woywod, Stanislaus, *A Practical Commentary on the Code of Canon Law*, 5. ed., 2 vols., New York: Wagner, 1939.

Principal Articles

Barin, Aloisius, "Commentarium ad Canones Iuris Canonici sacram Liturgiam Spectantes" — *Ephemerides Liturgicae*, XXXVIII (1924), 229-238; XXXIX (1925), 334-340.

Mahoney, E. J., "Reconciliation of Bombed Church"—*The Clergy Review*, XXI (1941), 116-117.

N. N., "Breviora Responsa"—*Ephemerides Liturgicae*, XXVII (1913), 676-677.

N. N., "De Ecclesia Violata"—*Promptuarium Canonico-Liturgicum*, reviewed in *Jus Pontificium*, IX (1929), 170.

O'Donnell, M. J., "Sacred Places and Sacred Times in the Code"—*The Irish Ecclesiastical Record*, 5th series, XIII (1919), 454-468.

Vermeersch, A., "De Consecratione, benedictione et reconciliatione Ecclesiae religiosorum"—*Periodica*, II (1911), 192-195.

Woywod, Stanislaus, "The Law of the Church on Sacred Places"—*HPR*, XXV (1925), 1079-1088.

Periodicals

Analecta Ecclesiastica (originally *Analecta Iuris Pontificii*, Romae: 1852-1868, Parisiis: 1869-1891), Romae: 1893-1911.

Clergy Review, The, London: 1931—

Collationes Brugenses, Brugis Flandrorum: 1896—

Ecclesiastical Review, The (originally *The American Ecclesiastical Review*), Philadelphia: 1889—

Ephemerides Liturgicae, Romae: 1886—

Homiletic and Pastoral Review, The, New York: 1900—

Irish Ecclesiastical Record, The, Dublin: 1864—

Jus Pontificium, Romae: 1921—

Le Canoniste (originally *Le Canoniste Contemporain*, 45 vols., Paris: 1878-1922), vols. 46-48, Paris: 1924-1926.

Nouvelle Revue Théologique, Paris: 1869—

Periodica de Re Canonica et Morali utili Praesertim Religiosis et Missionariis, Brugis: 1911—

Abbreviations

AAS—*Acta Apostolicae Sedis.*
AER—*American Ecclesiastical Review*
ASS—*Acta Sanctae Sedis.*
C. or c.—Canon.
Cc. or cc.—Canones.
Decr. Auth.—*Decreta Authentica.*
Fontes—*Codicis Iuris Canonici Fontes cura . . . Gasparri editi.*
Hardouin—*Acta Conciliorum etc.*
HPR—*Homiletic and Pastoral Review.*
Mansi—*Sacrorum Conciliorum Nova et Amplissima Collectio.*
MPG—Migne, *Patrologia Graeca.*
MPL—Migne, *Patrologia Latina.*
R.J.—*Regulae Iuris.*
S.C.C.—*Sacra Congregatio Concilii.*
S.C. Ep. et Reg.—*Sacra Congregatio Episcoporum et Regularium.*
S.C. Ep. et Reg.—*Sacra Congregatio Episcoporum et Regularium.*

BIOGRAPHICAL NOTE

John Theophilus Gulczynski was born August 26, 1911, in Wilmington, Delaware. His elementary and secondary education was received in the Catholic schools of that city. In the fall of 1928 he matriculated at SS. Cyril and Methodius Seminary at Orchard Lake, Michigan. He completed his theological studies at St. John's Seminary in San Antonio, Texas, and was ordained to the priesthood on June 7, 1936. The following three years he spent in parish work in the Diocese of Dallas. In September, 1939, he enrolled in the School of Canon Law at the Catholic University of America, where he received the degree of the Baccalaureate in Canon Law in June, 1940, and the degree of the Licentiate in Canon Law in June, 1941.

INDEX

CANON LAW STUDIES

1. Freriks, Rev. Celestine A., C.PP.S., J.C.D., Religious Congregations in Their External Relations, 121 pp., 1916.
2. Gallihcr, Rev. Daniel M., O.P., J.C.D., Canonical Elections, 117 pp., 1917.
3. Borkowski, Rev. Aurelius L., O.F.M., J.C.D., De Confraternitatibus Ecclesiasticis, 136 pp., 1918.
4. Castillo, Rev. Cayo, J.C.D., Disertacion Historico-Canonica sobre la Potestad del Cabildo en Sede Vacante o Impedida del Vicario Capitular, 99 pp., 1919 (1918).
5. Kubelbeck, Rev. William J., S.T.B., J.C.D., The Sacred Pentitentiaria and Its Relations to Faculties of Ordinaries and Priests, 129 pp., 1918.
6. Petrovits, Rev. Joseph J.C., S.T.D., J.C.D., The New Church Law On Matrimony, X-461 pp., 1919.
7. Hickey, Rev. John J., S.T.B., J.C.D., Irregularities and Simple Impediments in the New Code of Canon Law, 100 pp., 1920.
8. Klekotka, Rev. Peter J., S.T.B., J.C.D., Diocesan Consultors, 179 pp., 1920.
9. Wanenmacher, Rev. Francis, J.C.D., The Evidence in Ecclesiastical Procedure Affecting the Marriage Bond, 1920 (Printed 1935).
10. Golden, Rev. Henry Francis, J.C.D., Parochial Benefices in the New Code, IV-119 pp., 1921 (Printed 1925).
11. Koudelka, Rev. Charles J., J.C.D., Pastors, Their Rights and Duties According to the New Code of Canon Law, 211 pp., 1921.
12. Melo, Rev. Antonius, O.F.M., J.C.D., De Exemptione Regularium, X-188 pp., 1921.
13. Schaaf, Rev. Valentine Theodore, O.F.M., S.T.B., J.C.D., The Cloister, X-180 pp., 1921.
14. Burke, Rev. Thomas Joseph, S.T.D., J.C.D., Competence in Ecclesiastical Tribunals, IV-117 pp., 1922.
15. Leech, Rev. George Leo, J.C.D., A Comparative Study of the Constitution, "Apostolicae Sedis" and the "Codex Juris Canonici," 179 pp., 1922.
16. Motry, Rev. Hubert Louis, S.T.D., J.C.D., Diocesan Faculties According to the Code of Canon Law, II-167 pp., 1922.
17. Murphy, Rev. George Lawrence, J.C.D., Delinquencies and Penalties in the Administration and Reception of the Sacraments, IV-121 pp., 1923.
18. O'Reilly, Rev. John Anthony, S.T.B., J.C.D., Ecclesiastical Sepulture in the New Code of Canon Law, II-129 pp., 1923.

19. Michalicka, Rev. Wenceslas Cyrill, O.S.B., J.C.D., Judicial Procedure in Dismissal of Clerical Exempt Religious, 107 pp., 1923.
20. Dargin, Rev. Edward Vincent, S.T.B., J.C.D., Reserved Cases According to the Code of Canon Law, IV-103, pp., 1924.
21. Godfrey, Rev. John A., S.T.B., J.C.D., The Right of Patronage According to the Code of Canon Law, 153 pp., 1924.
22. Hagedorn, Rev. Francis Edward, J.C.D., General Legislation on Indulgences, II-154 pp., 1924.
23. King, Rev. James Ignatius, J.C.D., The Administration of the Sacraments to Dying Non-Catholics, V-141 pp., 1924.
24. Winslow, Rev. Francis Joseph, A.F.M., J.C.D., Vicars and Prefects Apostolic, IV-149 pp., 1924.
25. Correa, Rev. Jose Servelion, S.T.L., J.C.D., La Potestad Legislativa de la Iglesia Catolica, IV-127 pp., 1925.
26. Dugan, Rev. Henry Francis, A.M., J.C.D., The Judiciary Department of the Diocesan Curia, 87 pp., 1925.
27. Keller, Rev. Charles Frederick, S.T.B., J.C.D., Mass Stipends, 167 pp., 1925.
28. Paschang, Rev. John Linus, J.C.D., The Sacramentals According to the Code of Canon Law, 129 pp., 1925.
29. Pointek, Rev. Cyrillus, O.F.M., S.T.B., J.C.D., De Indulto Exclaustrationis necnon Saecularizationis, XIII-289 pp., 1925.
30. Kearney, Rev. Richard Joseph, S.T.B., J.C.D., Sponsors at Baptism According to the Code of Canon Law, IV-127 pp., 1925.
31. Bartlett, Rev. Chester Joseph, A.M., LL.B., J.C.D., The Tenure of Parochial Property in the United States of America, V-108 pp., 1926.
32. Kilker, Rev. Adrian Jerome, J.C.D., Extreme Unction, V-425 pp., 1926.
33. McCormick, Rev. Robert Emmett, J.C.D., Confessors of Religious, VIII-266 pp., 1926.
34. Miller, Rev. Newton Thomas, J.C.D., Founded Masses According to the Code of Canon Law, VII-93 pp., 1926.
35. Roelker, Rev. Edward G., S.T.D., J.C.D., Principles of Privilege According to the Code of Canon Law, XI-166 pp., 1926.
36. Bakalarczyk, Rev. Richardus, M.I.C., J.U.D., De Novitiatu, VIII-208 pp., 1927.
37. Pizzuti, Rev. Lawrence, O.F.M., J.U.L., De Parochis Religiosis, 1927. (Not printed).
38. Bliley, Rev. Nicholas Martin, O.S.B., J.C.D., Altars According to the Code of Canon Law, XIX-132 pp., 1927.
39. Brown, Mr. Brendan Francis, A.B. LL.M., J.U.D., The Canonical Juristic Personality with Special Reference to Its Status in the United States of America, V-212 pp., 1927.

40. Cavanaugh, Rev. William Thomas, C.P., J.U.D., The Reservation of the Blessed Sacrament, VIII-101 pp., 1927.
41. Doheny, Rev. William J., C.S.C., A.B., J.U.D., Church Property: Modes of Acquisition, X-118 pp., 1927.
42. Feldhaus, Rev. Aloysius H., C.PP.S., J.C.D., Oratories, IX-141 pp., 1927.
43. Kelly, Rev. James Patrick, A.B., J.C.D., The Jurisdiction of the Simple Confessor, X-208 pp., 1927.
44. Neuberger, Rev. Nicholas J., J.C.D., Canon 6 or the Relation of the Codex Juris Canonici to the Preceding Legislation, V-95 pp., 1927.
45. O'Keefe, Rev. Gerald Michael, J.C.D., Matrimonial Dispensations, Powers of Bishops, Priests and Confessors, VIII-232 pp., 1927.
46. Quigley, Rev. Joseph A.M., A.B., J.C.B., Condemned Societies, 139 pp., 1927.
47. Zaplotnik, Rev. Johannes Leo, J.C.D., De Vicariis Foraneis, X-142 pp., 1927.
48. Duskie, Rev. John Aloysius, A.B., J.C.D., The Canonical Status of the Orientals in the United States, VIII-196 pp., 1928.
49. Hyland, Rev. Francis Edward, J.C.D., Excommunication, Its Nature, Historical Development and Effects, VIII-181 pp., 1928.
50. Reinmann, Rev. Gerald Joseph, O.M.C., J.C.D., The Third Order Secular of Saint Francis, 201 pp., 1928.
51. Schenk, Rev. Francis J., J.C.D., The Matrimonial Impediments of Mixed Religion and Disparity of Cult, XVI-318 pp., 1929.
52. Coady, Rev. John Joseph, S.T.D., J.U.D., A.M., The Appointment of Pastors, VIII-150 pp., 1929.
53. Kay, Rev. Thomas Henry, J.C.D., Competence in Matrimonial Procedure, VIII-164 pp., 1929.
54. Turner, Rev. Sidney Joseph, C.P., J.U.D., The Vow of Poverty, XLIX-217 pp., 1929.
55. Kearney, Rev. Raymond, A., A.B., S.T.D., J.C.D., The Principles, of Delegation, VII-149 pp., 1929.
56. Conran, Rev. Edward James, A.B., J.C.D., The Interdict, V-163 pp., 1930.
57. O'Neil, Rev. William H., J.C.D., Papal Rescripts of Favor, VII-218 pp., 1930.
58. Bastnagel, Rev. Clement Vincent, J.U.D., The Appointment of Parochial Adjutants and Assistants, XV-257 pp., 1930.
59. Ferry, Rev. William A., A.B., J.C.D., Stole Fees. V-135 pp., 1930.
60. Costello, Rev. John Michael, A.B., J.C.D., Domicile and Quasi-domicile, VII-201 pp., 1930.
61. Kremer, Rev. Michael Nicholas, A.B., S.T.B., J.C.D., Church Support in the United States, VI-1930.

62. Angulo, Rev. Luis, C.M., J.C.D., Legislation de la Iglesia sobre la intencion en la application de la Santa Misa, VII-104 pp., 1931.
63. Frey, Rev. Wolfgang Norbert, O.S.B., A.B., J.C.D., The Act of Religious Profession, VIII-174 pp., 1931.
64. Roberts, Rev. James Brendan, A.B., J.C.D., The Banns of Marriage, XIV-140 pp., 1931.
65. Ryder, Rev. Raymond Aloysius, A.B., J.C.D., Simony, IX-151 pp., 1931.
66. Campagna, Rev. Angelo, Ph.D., J.U.D., Il Vicario Generale del Vescovo, VII-205 pp., 1931.
67. Cox, Rev. Joseph Godfrey, A.B., J.C.D., The Administration ot Seminaries, VI-124 pp., 1931.
68. Gregory, Rev. Donald J., J.U.D., The Pauline Privilege, XV-165 pp., 1931.
69. Donohue, Rev. John F., J.C.D., The Impediment of Crime, VII-110 pp., 1931.
70. Dooley, Rev. Eugene A., O.M.I., J.C.D., Church Law On Sacred Relics, IX-143 pp., 1931.
71. Orth, Rev. Raymond Clement, O.M.C., J.C.D., The Approbation of Religious Institutes, 171 pp., 1931.
72. Pernicone, Rev. Joseph M., A.B., J.C.D., The Ecclesiastical Prohibition of Books, XII-267 pp., 1932.
73. Clinton, Rev. Connell, A.B., J.C.D., The Paschal Precept, IX-108 pp., 1932.
74. Donnelly, Rev. Francis B., A.M., S.T.L., J.C.D., The Diocesan Synod, VIII-125 pp., 1932.
75. Torrente, Rev. Camilo, C.M.F., J.C.D., Las Processiones Sagradas, V-145 pp., 1932.
76. Murphy, Rev. Edwin J., C.PP.S., J.C.D., Suspension Ex Informata Conscientia, XI-122, pp., 1932.
77. Mackenzie, Rev. Eric F., A.M., S.T.L., J.C.D., The Delict of Heresy in its Commission Penalization, Absolution, VII-124 pp., 1932.
78. Lyons Rev. Avitus E., S.T.B., J.C.D., The Collegiate Tribunal of First Instance, XI-147 pp., 1932.
79. Connolly, Rev. Thomas A., J.C.D., Appeals, XI-195 pp., 1932.
80. Sangmeister, Rev. Joseph V., A.B., J.C.D., Force and Fear as Precluding Matrimonial Consent, V-211 pp., 1932.
81. Jaeger, Rev. Leo A., A.B., J.C.D., The Administration of Vacant and Quasi-vacant Episcopal Sees in the United States, IX-229 pp., 1932.
82. Rimlinger, Rev. Herbert T., J.C.D., Error Invalidating Matrimonial Consent, VII-79 pp., 1932.
83. Barrett, Rev. John D.M., S.S., J.C.D., A Comparative Study of the Third Plenary Council of Baltimore and the Code, IX-221 pp., 1932.

84. Carberry, Rev. John J., Ph.D., S.T.D., J.C.D., The Juridical Form of Marriage, X-177 pp., 1934.
85. Dolan, Rev. John L., A.B., J.C.D., The Defensor Vinculi, XII-157 pp., 1934.
86. Hannan, Rev. Jerome D., A.M., S.T.D., LL.B., J.C.D., The Canon Law of Wills, IX-517 pp., 1934.
87. Lemieux, Rev. Delisle A., A.M., J.C.D., The Sentence in Ecclesiastical Procedure, IX-131 pp., 1934.
88. O'Rourke, Rev. James J., A.B., J.C.D., Parish Registers, VII-109 pp., 1934.
89. Timlin, Rev. Bartholomew, O.F.M., A.M., J.C.D., Conditional Matrimonial Consent, X-381 pp., 1934.
90. Wahl, Rev. Francis X., A.B., J.C.D., The Matrimonial Impediments of Consanguinity and Affinity, VI-125 pp., 1934.
91. White, Rev. Robert J., A.B., LL.B., S.T.B., J.C.D., Canonical Ante-Nuptial Promises and the Civil Law, VI-152 pp., 1934.
92. Herrera, Rev. Antonio Parra, O.C.D., J.C.D., Legislation Ecclesiastica sobra el Ayuno y la Abstinencia, XI-191 pp., 1935.
93. Kennedy, Rev. Edwin J., J.C.D., The Special Matrimonial Process in Cases of Evident Nullity, X-165 pp., 1935.
94. Manning, Rev. John J., A.B., J.C.D., Presumption of Law in Matrimonial Procedure, XI-111 pp., 1935.
95. Moeder, Rev. John M., J.C.D., The Proper Bishop for Ordination and Dismissorial Letters, VII-135 pp., 1935.
96. O'Mara, Rev. William A., A.B., J.C.D., Canonical Causes For Matrimonial Dispensations, IX-155 pp., 1935.
97. Reilly, Rev. Peter, J.C.D., Residence of Pastors, IX-81 pp., 1935.
98. Smith, Rev. Mariner T., O.P., S.T.L., J.C.D., The Penal Law For Religious, VII-169 pp., 1935.
99. Whalen, Rev. Donald W., A.M., J.C.D., The Value of Testimonial Evidence in Matrimonial Procedure, XIII-297 pp., 1935.
100. Cleary, Rev. Joseph F., J.C.D., Canonical Limitations on the Alienation of Church Property, VIII-141 pp., 1936.
101. Glynn, Rev. John C., J.C.D., The Promoter of Justice, XX-337 pp., 1936.
102. Brennan, Rev. James H., S.S., A.M., S.T.B., J.C.D., The Simple Convalidation of Marriage, VI-135 pp, 1937.
103. Brunini, Rev. Joseph Bernard, J.C.D., The Clerical Obligations of Canons, 139 and 142, X-121 pp., 1937.
104. Connor, Rev. Maurice, A.B., J.C.D., The Administrative Removal of Pastors, VIII-159 pp., 1937.
105. Guilfoyle, Rev. Merlin Joseph, J.C.D., Custom, XI-144 pp., 1937.
106. Hughes, Rev. James Austin, A.B., A.M., J.C.D., Witnesses in Criminal Trials of Clerics, IX-140 pp., 1937.

107. Jansen, Rev. Raymond J., A.B., S.T.L., J.C.D., Canonical Provisions for Catechetical Instruction, VII-153 pp., 1937.
108. Kealy, Rev. John James, A.B., J.C.D,, The Introductory Libellus in Church Court Procedure, XI-121 pp., 1937.
109. McManus, Rev. James Edward, C.SS.R., J.C.D., The Administration of Temporal Goods in Religious Institutes, XVI-196 pp., 1937.
110. Moriarity, Rev. Eugene James, J.C.D., Oaths in Ecclesiastical Courts, X-115 pp., 1937.
111. Rainer, Rev. Eligius George, C.SS.R., J.C.D., Suspension of Clerics, XVII-249 pp., 1937.
112. Reilly, Rev. Thomas F., C.SS.R., J.C.D., Visitation of Religious, VI-195 pp., 1938.
113. Moriarty, Rev. Francis E., C.SS.R., J.C.D., The Extraordinary Absolution from Censures, XV-334 pp., 1938.
114. Connolly, Rev. Nicholas P., J.C.D., The Canonical Erection of Parishes, X-132 pp., 1938.
115. Donovan, Rev. James Joseph, J.C.D., The Pastor's Obligation in Prenuptial Investigation, VII-322 pp., 1938.
116. Harrigan, Rev. Robert J., M.A., S.T.B., J.C.D., The Radical Sanation of Invalid Marriages, VIII-208 pp., 1938.
117. Boffa, Rev. Conrad Humbert, J.C.D., Canonical Provisions for Catholic Schools, VII-211 pp., 1939.
118. Parsons, Rev. Anscar John, O.M. Cap., J.C.D., Canonical Elections, XII-236 pp., 1939.
119. Reilly, Rev. Edward Michael, A.B., J.C.D., The General Norms of Dispensation, X-156 pp., 1939.
120. Ryan, Rev. Gerald Aloysius, A.B., J.C.D., Principles of Episcopal Jurisdiction, XII-172 pp., 1939.
121. Burton, Rev. Francis James, C.S.C., A.B., J.C.D., A Commentary on Canon 1125, X-222 pp., 1940.
122. Miaskiewicz, Rev. Francis Sigismund, J.C.D., Supplied Jurisdiction according to Canon 209, XII-340 pp., 1940.
123. Rice, Rev. Patrick William, A.B., J.C.D., Proof of Death in Prenuptial Investigation, VIII-156 pp., 1940.
124. Anglin, Rev. Thomas Francis, M.S., J.C.D., The Eucharistic Fast, VIII-183 pp., 1941.
125. Coleman, Rev. John Jerome, J.C.D., The Minister of Confirmation, VI-153 pp., 1941.
126. Downs, Rev. John Emmanuel, A.B., J.C.D., The Concept of Clerical Immunity.
127. Esswein, Rev. Anthony Albert, J.C.D., Extrajudicial Penal Powers of Ecclesiastical Superiors, X-144 pp., 1941.

128. Farrell, Rev. Benjamin Francis, M.A., S.T.L., J.C.D., The Rights and Duties of the Local Ordinary Regarding Congregations of Women Religious of Pontifical Approval, V-195 pp., 1941.
129. Feeney, Rev. Thomas John, A.B., S.T.L., J.C.D., Restitution in Integrum, VI-169 pp., 1941.
130. Findlay, Rev. Stephen William, O.S.B., A.B., J.C.D., Canonical Norms Governing the Deposition and Degradation of Clerics.
131. Goodwine, Rev. John, A.B., S.T.L., J.C.D., The Right of the Church to Acquire Property, VIII-119 pp., 1941.
132. Heston, Rev. Edward Louis, C.S.C., PhD., S.T.D., J.C.D., The Alienation of Church Property in the United States, XII-222 pp., 1941.
133. Hogan, Rev. James John, S.T.L., J.C.D., Judicial Advocates and Procurators, VIII-200 pp., 1941.
134. Kealy, Rev. Thomas M. A.B., Litt.B., J.C.D., Dowry of Women Religious, IX-152 pp., 1941.
135. Keene, Rev. Michael James, O.S.B., J.C.D., Religious Ordinaries and Canon 198.
136. Kerin, Rev. Charles A., S.S., M.A., S.T.B., J.C.D., The Privation of Christian Burial, XVI-279 pp., 1941.
137. Louis, Rev. William Francis, M.A., J.C.D., Diocesan Archives, X-101 pp., 1941.
138. McDevitt, Rev. Gilbert Joseph, A.B., J.C.D., Legitimacy and Legitimation.
139. McDonough, Rev. Thomas Joseph, A.B., J.C.D., Apostolic Administrators.
140. Meier, Rev. Carl Anthony, A.B., J.C.D., Penal Administrative Procedure Against Negligent Pastors, XI-240 pp., 1941.
141. Schmidt, Rev. John Rogg, A.B., J.C.D., The Principles of Authentic Interpretation in Canon 17 of the Code of Canon Law, XII-331 pp., 1941.
142. Slafkosky, Rev. Andrew eLonard, A.B., J.C.D., The Canonical Episcopal Visitation of the Diocese, X-197 pp., 1941.
143. Swoboda, Rev. Innocent Robert, O.F.M., J.C.D., Ignorance in Relation to the Imputability of Delicts, IX-271 pp., 1941.
144. Dubé, Rev. Arthur Joseph, A.B., J.C.D., The General Principles for the Reckoning of Time in Canon Law. VIII-299 pp., 1941.
145. McBride, Rev. James T., A.B., J.C.D., Incardination and Excardination of Seculars., XX-585 pp., 1941.
146. Król, Rev. John J., J.C.L., The Defendant in Contentious Trials, IX-207 pp., 1942.
147. Comyns, Rev. Joseph J., C.SS.R., J.C.L., The Papal and Episcopal Administration of Church Property.
148. Barry, Rev. Garrett Francis, O.M.I., J.C.L., Violation of the Cloister.

149. Bolduc, Rev. Gatien, C.S.V., A.B., S.T.L., J.C.L., Les études dans les religions cléricales.
150. Boyle, Rev. David John, M.A., J.C.L., The Juridic Effects of Moral Certitude on Pre-Nuptial Guarantees.
151. Canavan, Rev. Walter Joseph, M.A., Litt.D., J.C.L., Profession of Faith.
152. Desrochers, Rev. Bruno, A.B., Ph.L., S.T.B., J.C.L., Le Premier Concile Plénier de Québec et le Code de Droit Canonique.
153. Dillon, Rev. Robert Edward, A.B., J.C.L., Common Law Marriage.
154. Dodwell, Rev. Edward John, Ph.D., S.T.B., J.C.L., The Time and Place for the Celebration of Marriage.
155. Donnellan, Rev. Thomas Andrew, A.B., J.C.L., The Obligation of the Missa pro Populo.
156. Eltz, Rev. Louis Anthony, A.B., JC.L., Cooperation in Crime.
157. Gass, Rev. Sylvester Francis, M.A., J.C.L., Ecclestiastical Pensions.
158. Guiniven, Rev. John Joseph, C.SS.R., J.C.L., The Precept of Hearing Mass on Sundays and Holy Days of Obligation.
159. Gulczynski, Rev. John Theophilus, J.C.L., The Desecration and Violation of Churches.
160. Hammill, Rev. John Leo, M.A., J.C.L., The Obligations of the Traveler according to Canon 14.
161. Haydt, Rev. John Joseph, A.B., J.C.L., Reserved Benefices.
162. Huser, Rev. Roger John, O.F.M., A.B., J.C.L., The Crime of Abortion in Canon Law.
163. Kearney, Rev. Francis Patrick, A.B., S.T.L., J.C.L., The Principles of Canon 1127.
164. Linahen, Rev. Leo James, S.T.L., J.C.L., De Absolutione Complicis in Peccato Turpi.
165. McCloskey, Rev. Joseph Aloysius, A.B., J.C.L., The Subject of Ecclesiastical Law according to Canon 12.
166. O'Neill, Rev. Francis Joseph, C.SS.R., J.C.L., The Dismissal of Religious in Temporary Vows.
167. Prince, Rev. John Edward, A.B., S.T.B., J.C.L., The Diocesan Chancellor.
168. Riesner, Rev. Albert Joseph, C.SS.R., J.C.L., Apostates and Fugitives from Religious Institutes.
169. Stenger, Rev. Joseph Bernard, J.C.L., The Mortgaging of Church Property.
170. Waldron, Rev. Joseph Francis, A.B., J.C.L., The Minister of Baptism.
171. Willett, Rev. Robert Albert, J.C.L., The Probative Value of Documents in Ecclesiastical Trials.
172. Woeber, Rev. Edward Martin, M.A., J.C.L., The Interpellations.

www.ingramcontent.com/pod-product-compliance
Lightning Source LLC
LaVergne TN
LVHW050208080826
844660LV00012B/376

* 9 7 8 0 8 1 3 2 2 3 4 8 3 *